I0158459

THE OLD
Waldorf-Astoria
BAR BOOK

Although each page was copied from the original edition, this reprint is in no way endorsed by or associated with the Waldorf-Astoria. We hope for their continued success.

Since this was copied from a very very old original edition, the pages here may look a little funny at times. Rest assured we did our best to format the original book into modern form as best allowed by the current processes available.

Introduction and Cover Art Copyright 2018 – All rights reserved.

INTRODUCTION

Welcome to "The Old Waldorf Astoria Bar Book 1935 Reprint".

The Old Waldorf hotel was built next door to William Astor's aunt, on the present day spot of the Empire State Building, because of a dispute with her. When she moved uptown the Old Waldorf hotel joined with the Astoria hotel by a structure known as Peacock Alley, becoming eventually one entity.

The Waldorf-Astoria had a rich history because of the forward thinking devices, such as allowing women to enter unescorted, thus enabling the hotel to become a female society hotspot.

Their food was popularized by Oscar Tschirky, also known as "Oscar of the Waldorf", who claimed creation for Eggs Benedict, Waldorf Salad (apples, celery, walnuts), and Veal Oscar.

As for drinks, the Waldorf-Astoria is said to have created the Bronx and popularized the Old Fashioned.

Forget about bar bibles or encyclopedias, what about drinks that people really used? This 1935 bar guide and bartender's recipe book is special as it was written right after prohibition about the drinks that would be served to famous people of the time.

Luckily, A.S. Crockett includes a wonderfully humorous history of the hotel's bar and a historical view of how drink recipes changed before and after prohibition.

As so few bar books were written and even fewer survived at all from the past 100 years, it a great pleasure to be able to bring these drinks that were used by the famous bar to our modern attention and use.

-Ross Bolton
December 3, 2018

THE OLD
Waldorf-Astoria
BAR BOOK

———•———

WITH AMENDMENTS DUE TO
REPEAL OF THE XVIIITH

———•———

Giving the Correct Recipes for FIVE HUNDRED COCKTAILS
and MIXED DRINKS known and served at the World's Most
Famous Brass Rail before Prohibition, together with More
than ONE HUNDRED ESTABLISHED FORMULAS for Cocktails
and Other Beverages, Originated while
Prohibition was in Effect

———•———

*The Whole Flavored with Dashes of History
Mixed in a Shaker of Anecdote and Served with a
Chaser of Illuminative Information*

BY

ALBERT STEVENS CROCKETT
(HISTORIAN OF THE OLD WALDORF-ASTORIA)
Illustrations by Leighton Budd

A. S. CROCKETT
NEW YORK   1935

RECALLING

CERTAIN GENTLEMEN OF OTHER DAYS,
WHO MADE OF DRINKING
ONE OF THE PLEASURES OF LIFE —
NOT ONE OF ITS EVILS;
WHO ACHIEVED CONTENT
LONG ERE CAPACITY
WAS REACHED OR OVERTAXED;
AND
WHO, WHATEVER THEY DRANK,
PROVED ABLE TO CARRY IT,
KEEP THEIR HEADS
AND REMAIN GENTLEMEN,
EVEN IN THEIR CUPS
THEIR EXAMPLE
IS COMMENDED
TO THEIR
POSTERITY

CONTENTS

THE OLD
𝕎𝕒𝕝𝕕𝕠𝕣𝕗-𝔸𝕤𝕥𝕠𝕣𝕚𝕒
BAR BOOK

THE BAR OF THE OLD WALDORF

I. PREAMBULARY

DURING what facetious American newspaper column-
ists sometimes referred to as the Period of the
Great Drought—that is to say, during the days of the
Noble Experiment—the art of mixing cocktails as known
and practiced up to 1919 lapsed into a sort of desuetude,
even if that could not be described as "innocuous" or even
as innoxious.

In those larger times when legal liquor could be had
more or less freely in this country, if one had the price,
or was fortunate enough to be declared in by some host
standing treat, new drinks owed their invention either to
unusually enterprising barmen, or to customers gifted with
imagination and longing for new savors and flavors or,
possibly, the inspiration was attributable to what they had
already drunk. Here and there one knew some amateur
experimenter whose chief indoor sport was putting together
new and sometimes weird and even terrifying concoctions
and trying the result upon his friends. During the decade
and a half preceding the Great War, "Have you tried
this one?" was almost as frequent a prelude to something
as "Have you heard this one?"

The war in Europe definitely diminished creative activities in the cocktail line. From London we heard that
Britishers, drawn into the combat, had taken to drinking
champagne, and were even being weaned away from their
Scotch. When the A.E.F. discovered France, a simul-
taneous discovery was made of the wines of the country,

together with what was quantitatively described as *"beau-coup cognac."* When the survivors of the War and its attendant gustatory campaigns got back home, it was to a country all set for strict Constitutional sobriety, legally enforced. America was to be dried up.

Of course, no such thing happened, except in theory. Sumptuary legislation has always proved repugnant to free men and difficult to enforce. Instead of becoming alcoholically arid, the United States grew wetter and wetter as the years passed. The bootlegger, once among the most despised members of society, became important—as important in his way as the Missing Link might be considered by ethnologists and anthropologists of the Darwinian school. Indeed, he proved a missing link. He bought magnificent motor cars or high speed motor boats, amassed fortunes, grew into might and acquired a definite and even respectable status as an indispensable member of society. More than one read his name in some Social Roster, —though it had probably been printed there before he turned outlaw. The racketeer and the gangster, protected by the politician and even in collusion with the revenue officer, waxed powerful and became superior to the law. The average American who wanted liquor bought from one or the other. What he got was their business, not his. True, persons with long purses might purchase what was "good stuff" according to pre-war standards, but mistakes were made. The rest of us often paid fancy prices for labels. Stimulated by the very difficulties created by the law and encouraged by the ease with which those difficulties could be surmounted, as well as by the temptation to break a statute that was never popular in large centers of population, an appetite for strong drink spread among the young, not sparing young women. It became "smart" to affect the speakeasy and to make it a place of assemblage; and "drunk" and "souse" became humorous rather than disreputable terms.

But avast with moral discussions! The story has been written, and we are trying to recover from what in effect was a national spree—with headaches, and sometimes worse. The fact was that, deprived of legal liquor, we had embarked, as it were, upon an unknown sea of alcoholic beverages. Thirsts were drowned, rather than quenched, in "bathtub" or synthetic gin—that or "whiskey" made from supposedly denatured wood-alcohol. Fatalities were frequent. The cocktail, long considered an aid to good appetite and digestion and cheer, often proved an enemy to digestion, health, morals and even mind. In sum, the art of drinking, according to the tenets of the long established American School, was lost, except one found in Havana, or Nassau, or elsewhere abroad, some veteran barman whose training and experience qualified him to compose drinks in the old, standard American way. The men employed in speakeasies to mix cocktails and other drinks as a rule knew nothing about the job and did not have valid liquors to start with. A "cocktail" was apt to prove just something with so-called gin in it, or a mixture of two or more of the imitations that masked behind well-known names.

Self-respecting bartenders of the old day—or most of them—had found other means of earning a living. Some had emigrated. There were exceptions. Breaking the law of the land—a frequent avocation for many of us—most of our social clubs found employment for experienced barmen. But rare it was that this particular searcher for truth and good spirit, who, through the courtesy of friends was enabled to sample the offerings of many club bars, tasted a cocktail that seemed authentic. And he never drank a cocktail at a club bar during the prohibition era without wondering whether it would prove his last.

Neighboring countries benefited much from prohibition in the United States. For Canada the Yankee tourist trade proved a great boon. From early spring to late autumn the roads carried northward hosts of automobilists, bent, not upon seeing the natural and other wonders of the Dominion so much as on sampling the spirituous fare available to any comer. Usually their first port of call, once across the border, or after registering at a hotel, was a government liquor store, which exhibited a generous desire to accommodate, despite the legal limitations on sales to a single customer. All one had to do was to go back as early and as often as he pleased. A late afternoon in a Montreal hotel usually yielded ebullient evidence of a heavy American invasion, which proclaimed to all within ear-shot that it had got what it had come for.

Certain steamship companies finally awoke to the possibilities that lay in catering particularly to our denied and increasing demand for good liquor and plenty of it; and week-end cruises, swift turn-about jaunts to the tropics and return "voyages to Nowhere" won enormous popularity and helped erase some of the "red ink" into which the trans-Atlantic steamship companies had sunk until they were almost awash. Many who embarked on such cruises later yielded curious descriptions of the foreign ports they had visited, telling of a Havana that was paved with sawdust and contained mostly within "Sloppy Joe's"; and a tour of the British West Indies often seemed to linger in memory mostly as a series of dashes from a table to the bar of "Dirty Dick's," in Nassau. It came to be said that a ship's company in those days did not disembark upon arriving back in New York, but was poured out upon the pier.

When the repeal of the prohibition amendment was accomplished, on December 5, 1933, proprietors of New York hotels and restaurants made the discovery that good bartenders, men who knew anything at all about mixing cocktails, were scarce. Most of the old-timers had died off, or forgotten what they had known. Steamships and clubs were raided; barmen were even imported; but it is a good hazard that out of every ten men employed to mix cocktails on that historic day of Repeal, not more than one really knew the rudiments of his trade. Schools for bartenders had sprung up, but they could not turn out experts fast enough to qualify. Properly mixing a wide variety of cocktails requires much more than a month of training. Long practice is absolutely essential.

Besides, even in pre-prohibition days, no one man could keep all the drink recipes in his head. Few latter-day cocktail slingers really have any conception of the number and variety of cocktails and other mixed drinks that used to be in demand. In order to be able to serve the correct cocktail when a customer called for his fancy of the moment, recipes had been written down and kept ready for consultation.

During the last few years, the market has been flooded with so-called cocktail recipe books. Without challenging them all, one may mention that some seem to have been based on the practices and even on the orthography of speakeasy "bar-keeps." In one, for example, I came across

the recipe for a "Dacqueri"—presumably intended for "Daiquiri," but whose formula would not be recognized as such
anywhere in Cuba, where the rum it contains is the national
drink. Not long ago, I made an examination of one
volume which, judging from the quantity of names dis-
played, offered a tremendous number of cocktail recipes
of startling variety. I found fewer than seventy whose
names and formulas were known to me. Out of that seventy, the recipes for not as many as ten agreed with the
formulas of pre-war times that were in my possession. They
brought up Pickwickian memories.

"It depends, my lord," said *Mr. Weller,* during the
trial of Bardell *vs.* Pickwick, "upon the taste and fancy of
the speller."

Back in softer-boiled days and for more than twenty
years, New York boasted many well run and well known
bars, and one in particular that was famous all over the
world. Everybody from everywhere who wanted the best
of drinks, made according to the best traditions of the
American School, found his way to it when he reached
New York and carried away memories of it. In far-off
Shanghai, in Peking, in Singapore, in Melbourne, in Cape-
town, in Johannesburg, in Aden, in Calcutta, an American traveler was sure to find in a local club or hotel
somebody who would boast of having had such-and-such
a cocktail in the Old Waldorf-Astoria Bar. If the new acquaintance was a Scot, he was apt to lick reminiscent chops
over the generous free lunch there dispensed.

The barmen in that historic dispensary—an even dozen
of them when good times made good business—had to
know what was what when it came to mixing and serving drinks. As at most first class bars of the period, all

recipes were written down once they had been invented and tasted. Every new recipe brought to the bar must pass a try-out before it was inscribed in the Bar Book. It is to the fact that one of the Old Waldorf barmen held on to the copy of that Bar Book long after prohibition had shut what had grown by repute to the dignity of an American institution that we owe the preservation of the names and the real recipes of the authentic cocktails and most of the recognized mixed alcoholic drinks of ante-prohibition days. That barman was Joseph Taylor, who had been "called to the Bar" during its early days and who helped close it. He remained in the employ of the Old Waldorf-Astoria until its last day, working in what became known as its "beverage department" and handling no more stimulating potations than aerated water, ginger ale and near-beer. After the old hotel was closed, in 1929, Taylor was out of a job for a time, finally obtaining precarious employment until the opening of the new Waldorf. His self-respect would not permit him to work in a speakeasy, he told me. He used to call upon me at intervals. The last time was about ten months before Repeal Day. He was then looking forward eagerly, he said, to the return of old times, and to getting back behind a counter and plying the cocktail shaker in the old way, with "real stuff" to pour into it from genuinely labeled bottles. But he did not live to see that day.

The Old Waldorf Bar Book he had given me to use as I saw fit when I was writing the history of the Old Waldorf Bar—which I had known from shortly after its opening until the end—and in it I incorporated the contents of the recipe book. That book was intended simply as a contribution to the social history of an age—one I had treated from other standpoints in another volume, PEACOCKS ON PARADE, earlier published. When OLD WAL-DORF BAR DAYS came out, few Americans dreamed that repeal was hardly more than two years off. And so, while I "translated" and more or less codified and put into alphabetical order the contents of that battered, dog-eared little album, its pages stained with many samples of liquors, and which would probably show under a microscope the thumb prints of many barmen who had had to consult it, I had no idea of turning out a guide of any sort. I merely incorporated it as something that might interest the researcher into American *mores*, who, I felt sure, would find much material therein, and so permitted myself very little elaboration.

However, the book attracted wide and favorable comment. As Repeal Day approached, critics and connoisseurs who knew good liquors and particularly what cocktails used to be like, found that, by virtue of having been long in actual daily use, here was an authoritative compendium of the authentic cocktails of a by-gone day. True, its availability was handicapped by being tacked on, as it were, to a quasi-historical narrative and exposition, so that those who merely saw the book and the title did not readily guess, as a rule, that it contained a collection of cocktail recipes. Because of the book's history, it stood alone. It should be improved, amplified as much as necessary, and made thoroughly understandable and useful.

This was emphasized by Mr. Howard L. Lewis, Secretary of Dodd, Mead and Company. So that the author, encouraged and stimulated by the interest of a publishing firm of such high reputation and standing, gladly undertook the work of revision.

Besides the revised formulas for cocktails and other mixed drinks contained in the Old Waldorf Bar Book, I have included a number of recipes for other standard cocktails and mixed drinks, mostly gathered outside of the United States, and many of them tested and approved by the author.

II. CONSTITUTIVE AND DERIVATIVE

THE cocktail, as many generations have known it, is a distinctively American drink. Its name, its formulas and its influence as well, have been spread by traveling Americans to every corner of the globe. Or else Britons, bound for some distant part of an empire on which the sun is always setting, learned a recipe in an American bar and made the barman at the club in their remote destination experiment until he had achieved something like the flavors of the mixture whose tastes and effects they longed to experience again.

At home—in London, or wherever he dwelt in his tight little island—the Englishman as a rule did not succumb easily to the innovation. For many years the fact that the cocktail was an American drink was sufficient to condemn it in his eyes. The Britisher stuck to his Sherry or his Scotch or Brandy-and-Soda. So that the spread of the cocktail in anything like its pristine purity, so to speak, was due in greatest measure to peripatetic Yankees, some of whom never found any strange place liveable, or even bearable, unless or until they could get their cocktails when they wanted them.

Not until the present century was ending its second decade was it possible anywhere in the London the compiler of this volume knew—and that was considerable— to buy a genuine cocktail made in the American way. In Paris, yes. The French, making early discovery that profit lurked in catering to thirsts hostile to claret or Burgundy, imported cocktail shakers and increased the manufacture of ice. Not a few Frenchmen had learned about cocktails in America. The Chatham bar and Henry's and a dozen or more other places knew just how Martinis and Old-Fashioneds were made, and served them. That was one reason why many an American found Paris more enjoyable than London, and stayed longer. Of course, in London hotel bars frequented by Americans, cocktails, so-called, were served long ago by English barmaids and drunk liberally. American visitors, though they refused to acquire the tea habit and balked at Scotch, simply had to drink something in that climate. But somehow the concoctions lacked authenticity; they did not taste like real cocktails. English bartenders and barmaids, it appeared, found as much difficulty composing cocktails harmoniously as did their musicians in learning to play music of American origin and tempo. At this distance and with the conquest of London by our "jazz kings" a part of ancient history, the comparison must seem inept. But I knew the London of twenty-five to thirty years ago; I lived there.

Not until the summer of 1920, so far as I was able to ascertain, did an American-trained barman make his appearance at one of the high-class London hotels. That was the year when most American bartenders found themselves out of jobs. This one, however, was a Britisher. I knew the Englishman who had been commissioned by the management of that hotel to find such an expert in New York and happened to be in the lobby when the result of the mission was announced. I sampled one of the newcomer's first cocktails made on British soil.

Out in the Far East, the American Navy, true to tradition, did its share in spreading the gospel of the cocktail.

Certainly whatever may have been lacking in the results of their missionary endeavors up to the Spanish-American War was made up in 1898, just before and after Dewey's capture of the Spanish fleet in Manila Bay and during the Boxer Rebellion a few years later. Whatever the oft-encountered sign "American Bar" may have lacked in authentic backing when one encountered it in Europe, out in what were known as the Treaty Ports of China, in Yokohama and such other places in the Orient as our sailors, marines and soldiers came to know, one could find his Martini or any other cocktail that was in vogue back in the States.

Yet, while the cocktail is an American invention, its derivation and first date of application are hazed by anecdote and fancy. Take, for example, a story once heard in the Orient.

"A cocktail?" the Mandarin repeated, eying the drink doubtfully.

"Yes," replied the Standard Oil man, his host in Hong Kong.

"But why the name?"

The other shook his head. "Drink it and you will find the rooster feathers growing on you."

The Mandarin drank, perplexed. Having drunk, however, his curiosity over the name left him. All he wanted was another of the same. Soon afterward began in the Far East a demand for bottled Martinis and Manhattans, which did more to Americanize the Chinese than any other influence.

There was once a day when women did not drink cocktails. They even hesitated to pronounce the name. Over here we spoke of "roosters." Of course everybody knew that roosters had tails and it was a common opinion that the effect of a cocktail was to make the imbiber feel somehow like a rooster with his tail stuck up. Anyhow, if the cocktail was properly made, it had the effect of at least stimulating the appetite. But that much admitted, the derivation is still an open question and the date undecided.

As my habit, when at a loss for the origin of a word, is to appeal to one of the foremost lexicographers in our land, I put the ancestry of "cocktail" up to Dr. Frank H. Vizetelly, managing editor of the Standard Dictionary. Then it developed that even that eminent root specialist found himself stumped when it came to pinning an exact date on the word and getting down to the bottom of its family tree. But Dr. Vizetelly was kind enough to go into the matter with great thoroughness.

"The *cocktail*," Dr. Vizetelly replied, "goes back at least to the beginning of the 19th century, and may date back to the American Revolution. It is alleged by one writer to have been a concoction prepared by the widow of a Revolutionary soldier as far back as 1779. He offers no proof of the statement, but a publication, 'The Balance,' for May 13, 1806, describes the *cocktail* of that period as 'a stimulating liquor composed of spirits of any kind, sugar, water and bitters. It is vulgarly called "bitter sling," and is supposed to be an excellent electioneering potion.'

"Washington Irving, in 'Knickerbocker' (1809), Page 241, said of the cocktail: 'They (Dutch-Americans) lay claim to be the first inventors of the recondite beverages, cock-tail, stone-fence, and sherry cobbler.' Hawthorne referred to *cocktails* in 'The Blithedale Romance' (1852), as did Thackeray in his 'The Newcomes' (1855), but neither of these authors sheds any light upon the origin of the term.

"The New English Dictionary on Historical Principles says that the origin of the word *cocktail* is lost. In this connection, one writer refers to the older term *cocktail*, meaning a horse whose tail, being docked, sticks up like the tail of a cock. He adds: 'Since drinkers of cocktails believe them to be exhilarating, the recently popular song, "Horsey, keep your tail up," may perhaps hint at a possible connection between the two senses of "cocktail." '

"Bartlett in his 'Dictionary of Americanisms' gives the following: *'Cocktail'*—A stimulating beverage, made of brandy, gin or other liquor, mixed with bitters, sugar and very little water. A friend thinks that this term was suggested by the shape which froth, as of a glass of porter, assumes when it flows over the sides of a tumbler containing the liquid effervescing.' He quotes the following from the *New York Tribune* of May 8, 1862: 'A bowie-knife and a foaming cocktail.' In the Yorkshire dialect, *cocktail* described beer that is fresh and foaming.

"Brewer, in 'A Dictionary of Phrase and Fable,' following the definition of *cocktail*, adds the note: 'The origin of the term is unknown. The story given in the *New York World* (1891) to the effect that it is an Aztec word, and that 'the liquor' was discovered by an Aztec noble, who sent it by the hand of his daughter Xochitl to the King, who promptly named it "xoctl," whence "cocktail," is a good specimen of the manufacture of etymologies.'

"As you will see from the foregoing," Dr. Vizetelly concludes, "altho many theories have been advanced as to the etymology of the term *cocktail*, these, like most etymologies of the kind, are mere flights of fancy, and while they make interesting reading, can not be accepted as reliable."

So much for derivation and history. Now for the meaning of cocktail. The Standard Dictionary gives it as "[U. S.] A drink made of spirits mixed with bitters, sugar and flavor."

Well, that's sufficient to start with. But it was not a speakeasy definition during prohibition, and millions of Americans have grown up with very different ideas. In the Old Waldorf Bar Book, bitters of one kind or other was considered a necessary ingredient of most Gin cocktails. The favorite was Orange Bitters, which appears in something like one hundred different recipes. A distant second was Angostura. Then there were Calisaya, Boonekamp, Boker's, Amer Picon, Hostetter's, Pepsin, Peychaud, Fernet Branca, and so on. The Bitters was used in small quantities, ordinarily described as "one dash" or "two." But Bitters used to contain alcohol and prohibition made most brands illegal to import. One well known firm which specialized during prohibition in importing liquors whose alcoholic content had been reduced until they could be brought in as "flavoring extracts," told me it had not imported Orange Bitters in fourteen years.

The original Old Waldorf Bar Book contained almost three hundred cocktail recipes. That means more than appears, for of cocktails made with Vermouth there were frequently two variants, an ordinary and a "dry"—or "*sec.*" That was particularly true where the recipe called for Italian Vermouth. Using French Vermouth instead, the result was a "dry" cocktail, one that was not sweet and a better appetizer. Certain barmen claimed to make a dry cocktail simply by increasing the proportion of Gin.

Many recipes, however, call only for French Vermouth. Gin was the base, or one of the bases, of approximately one hundred and fifty cocktails—more if the "dry" variants of cocktails are considered as different entities. In making forty or so, Whiskey was the base. Rum of one sort or another was used only in fourteen; for Bacardi and Jamaica—though the latter was the favorite indulgence of many of our colonial forefathers—had not attained the wide acquaintance among Americans the latter now enjoy. In this book, Cuban and Jamaican drinks of today are taken up exhaustively following the contents of the Old Waldorf Bar Book. Sloe Gin was the base of eleven recipes. There were forty-four whose base was either Brandy or one of a number of cordials. Frequently two or more were mixed. Other bases were Applejack or Apple Brandy, Calisaya, Dubonnet, Sherry, Port and Swedish Punsch.

During the first two decades of the century, the commonly accepted American definition of a cocktail was a mixture of Gin and Vermouth with Bitters, iced and shaken. Of course, Whiskey cocktails had their many and ardent devotees; and the Manhattan, based on Whiskey, was a popular drink. To a big majority, however, Whiskey was something that should be taken neat, or, at most, adulterated with nothing more than water. In a highball, of course, the latter was aerated. The average Whiskey drinker regarded the mixture of good Bourbon or Rye with anything as a sort of sacrilege—except after the drink had gone down, when, as a rule, he liked to dispatch a small quantity of water in its wake. To many persons, Whiskey cocktails were so much medicine. To such, the ideal combination was Gin and Vermouth. Vermouth alone, as a drink, never won wide favor in this country, but it is noteworthy that more than half the cocktails known had Vermouth as an essential. Of them all, the favorite was the Dry Martini.

Undoubtedly the ancestor of the cocktail that gained widest vogue during prohibition, particularly among householders who had to make their own, was what was known both as the Adirondack and the Orange Blossom No. 2. It consisted of one-half Orange Juice and one-half Gin, and was served in a bar glass. In the period just past, many persons who thought they had dependable bootleggers made up a concoction that approached the Orange Blossom No. 1, which consisted of one-third Orange Juice, one-third Tom Gin and one-third Italian Vermouth; or else the Eddy, which was one-third Gordon Gin, one-third French Vermouth and one-third Orange Juice. When one's host served a Bronx, during the late Doubtful Drink Era, it was more apt to be something whose content was one of the three just named—or almost anything. As a rule, the Orange Juice, at least, was the "real stuff."

At this point it may be mentioned that between certain pairs of cocktails, the only difference lies in the brand of Gin used. Occasionally the only dissimilarity is in names. However, Shakespeare to the contrary, once in a while there was something in these, as will be shown later.

Despite a widely accepted belief that all cocktails were iced, there were exceptions to the general rule, as the recipes show. My personal preference is for an iced cocktail, and I always use a shaker, one that could hold much more than the quantity of ingredients used. To my notion, a good deal of muscle action is necessary in shaking properly, and one secret of a perfect cocktail is getting it to the drinker with the least possible delay; that is to say, like hot coffee, as soon as it is made.

Just where cocktails leave off and other mixed drinks begin it is difficult to determine. Some authorities would make cocktails all mixed drinks which have to be shaken—and cause dissensions. In reproducing the Old Waldorf Bar Book, I have followed in the main the classification of cocktails therein made. Many other mixed drinks fall into groups—determined, as a rule, by one or more of the ingredients used, or the method of making. Others can not be classified, and so are just listed alphabetically.

Before closing this dissertation on the products of the American School of Drinking, one must say frankly that so far as chemistry and logic are concerned, it would seem that either has had little to do with the formulas of most cocktails. The American School of Drinking, as it existed in other days, was never that of France; and so far as anybody has revealed, the rules of chemistry were never considered in arriving at formulas, nor was any dietitian consulted. Most American alcoholic concoctions exhibit little regard for chemistry, either in theory or application. In France, as Julian Street intimates in his "Wines," recently published, the art of drinking has, in a sense, been guided partly by the laws of chemical reactions. Generations of experts have determined which wines go best with certain foods; which aid the appetite or digestion. Moderation has usually been the keynote.

Americans, as a rule, drink partly for the taste, mostly for the effect. Those who prefer the effect to the taste like to get the same quickly. The cocktail, taken according to general practice, is not sipped as is wine. If it is not gulped, it is usually finished in three swallows, or at most four. Few of us on this side of the Atlantic, when we face

a cocktail, look for bouquets or aromas, to a French gour-
met among the most potent charms of wines and brandies.
Lots of Americans these days seem to like cocktails made
of two or more kinds of liqueurs. Such mixtures would
tend to shock the sophisticated foreigner, who has been
taught that anything of the nature of a liqueur should follow rather than precede a meal. Most American women
who acquired the cocktail habit while John Barleycorn was
doing time, judging from what one has seen in foreign
parts, prefer cocktails that are sweet, even if they are
strong. Indeed, during that now happily ended chapter
of American history, cocktail parties, which grew into
great vogue, were seldom intended to quicken the appetite
for dinner. They became occasions when intensive drinking was done and a provident host or hostess, aware that
hunger was bound to ensue, prided himself or herself upon
furnishing an abundant supply of *hors d'œuvres*, or, as
these came themselves to be known, "appetizers;" the result often being that persons who attended cocktail parties
preceding dinners so gorged themselves with these "delicate" but nevertheless substantial offerings, that by the
time they reached the dinner table they seldom had any
appetite left.

Moderation is the secret of enjoyment of anything, if
one wishes to retain the faculty for enjoyment. That rule
most certainly applies to cocktails and the whole category
of drink of any kind. And, according to very respectable
doctors, just as many digestive troubles originate from
over-eating as from too much drinking.

III. BAPTISMAL

THE visitor to a speakeasy, during the recent Period of Stress, may have lacked nothing in abundance of supply; but he was confronted by decided circumscription in variety. Had one who knew breathed to dispensers of dreadful drinks that masked under names once guarantees of superior content, and harmless, if potent, accelerators of appetite and good feeling—taken in moderation—some figures as well as facts about the quality and variety of alcoholic dispensation at the Old Waldorf in its real prime, he would probably have been greeted by a scouting or scornful, "Aw, what are ya givin' me?" Indeed, had you told almost anybody who hadn't the facts before him the number of kinds of fancy drinks Old Waldorf barmen knew how to concoct, and did concoct, they would have put you down as a liar and probably said it aloud.

Those three hundred or so varieties of what was once the great American drink, one which carried the name of our people all over the world; those over four hundred more varieties of picklers than the most ambitious American pickler of his age was ever able to advertise—and which pickled more people—deserve, with their formulas, to live in history. Their nomenclature belongs to it, not only as part of our national chronicles, but as an index to certain social, industrial and artistic achievements of an age.

Brushing aside such mythological, ornithological, theological, zoological, or otherwise "logical" designations as Adonis, Bird, Bridal, Bishop Poker, Creole, Goat's Delight, Gloom Lifter and Hoptoad—to name just a few samples of cocktails of other times—consider others that betray less of fancy and originality, but perhaps more of cause of origin.

For example, take the Armour, called after a well known Chicago patron of the establishment. Then there was a Beadleston, named after another customer who sold the Bar much of the beer he brewed, and after whom was baptized a second cocktail, the Beadleston No. 2. Speaking still alphabetically, there was a Bunyan, spelled with an "a," not an "o," and summoning up thoughts of a thirsty pilgrim's progress to a land of never-never-thirst. A "Chauncey" must have been named after the most distinguished person of that prenomen, a famous orator and wit. There is no record that its namesake was present at its christening. Nor is there evidence that the originator of a celebrated march upon Washington graced the birth of the Coxey cocktail. The Dorflinger got its name from a glass manufacturer who made containers for drinks.

For the creation of the Eddy, I may predicate at once that no scientific lady of that name was responsible; I am inclined to attribute its origin to a popular and handsome young diplomatist of the early part of the century who married an heiress and went into eclipse. And surely one would not think of attributing the Hearst cocktail to any personal interest on the part of a great newspaper proprietor; rather to certain of his staff who were in the habit of dropping in at odd times when assigned to a story in the neighborhood of what was then Herald Square.

And there was McKinley's Delight. Just why it was

McKinley's delight, 1 am unable to ascertain. The chances
are that President McKinley never found out whether it
was or not. In its favor, I may mention that the Bar was
a great hangout for the G.O.P.'s of yesteryear, who may
have passed their enthusiasm for their candidates across
the counter for the barman to translate into terms of liquid
intensity.

The Waldorf Bar served a Racquet Club, a Riding Club
and a Union League Club cocktail, thus honoring certain
social and representative New York institutions. But who
the "Mrs. Thompson" was, whose name was bestowed
upon one of its cocktails, frankly, I do not know. Nor do
I know just what state of spiritual or spirituous elevation,
or on whose part, suggested the christening of the St.
Francis or the St. Peter or the St. John, though the first
may have been called after a California hotel, and not
after a friar long deceased.

The stage, whether or not it drove men to drink in
those days, certainly inspired much drinking, and success-
ful plays often stood godfather for bartenders' concep-
tions. The great success of "Rosemary," with which John
Drew and one of Charles Frohman's best companies
helped open the Astoria part of the Old Waldorf-Astoria,
was celebrated in a cocktail of the same name, composed of
equal parts of Vermouth and Bourbon. The tuneful "Merry
Widow" and the almost equally whistleable "Chocolate
Soldier" were drowned in baptismal cocktails at the Waldorf Bar. The Merry Widow cocktail was made of half
French Vermouth and half Dubonnet; the Chocolate Soldier, an appropriately stronger potation, was composed
of one-third Dubonnet, two-thirds Nicholson Gin and a
dash of Lime Juice. "Peg o' My Heart" and "Rob Roy"

named other cocktails. "Trilby" had been drunk back in the days of the Waldorf sit-down Bar. In compliment to the locale of the play, the Trilby cocktail was made of one-third French Vermouth and two-thirds Old Tom Gin, with dashes of Orange Bitters and Crème Yvette. "Salomé," making a tremendous sensation in a single presentation at the Metropolitan Opera House, in 1907, was celebrated in a way that might have made Strauss weep for his seidel or his stein of Pilsner. With its two dashes of Absinthe, cementing half portions of Italian Vermouth and Dubonnet, the cocktail lacked German authorship, but certainly nothing in authority. Mrs. Leslie Carter must have heard, when she helped make David Belasco loom larger on the theatrical map, that "Zaza" made one of its biggest hits in the form of an invention of a Waldorf barman. The Zaza cocktail was somewhat milder than the Salomé, for only one-third of its content was Old Tom Gin, that being allied with two-thirds Dubonnet and two dashes of Orange Bitters. And Charlie Chaplin had a cocktail named in his honor when he began to make the screen public laugh.

In those days every big or spectacular event claimed its appropriate honorification at the hands of those Waldorf dispensers of drink. For example, the first composition of the Arctic cocktail celebrated Peary's discovery of the North Pole—or where it ought to be; the Doctor Cook cocktail proclaimed the exposure of a celebrated polar faker whose very entrails Peary once confessed to me personally, in effect, he hated; the invention of the Coronation cocktail was anticipative of the ten minutes' rest the late King Edward got when they sat him on the Stone of Scone. The Fin de Siècle came toward the end of the century, when the expression became current in magazines and newspapers, and when lots of Americans were taking their first steps in French. What they said when they meant to order such a cocktail is another matter.

Why, you can date many American historical, society, sporting, police and other events by those cocktails when you know the names. There was the Third Degree, invented when everybody in New York was interested in the way tough cops were extracting information from accused persons. Probably it left its imbiber in a state similar to that of the victim of a police inquisition. Added to one-eighth French Vermouth, it consisted of seven-eighths Plymouth Gin, with several dashes of Absinthe. The Good Times cocktail was reminiscent of the socially important coach that once ran from the Waldorf doorway to the Woodmansten Inn. The Jitney complimented an invention of a Detroit gentleman which was found adaptable to take the place of trolley cars when drivers and conductors went on strike. It may be particularly interesting to that inventor to learn that it was composed of one-half Gin, one-fourth Lemon, one-fourth Orange Juice—and a little Sugar. Then there was the Marconi Wireless, which first "materialized" at the Bar of the Old Waldorf when the ancestor of what is now called the "radio" began to raise its ghostly voice; and the Prince Henry, concocted to celebrate the arrival of the once-distinguished Kaiser's apostolic brother, who was dined and wined prodigiously in the old hotel's Grand Ballroom, just above the Barroom.

Cocktails by the names of Futurity, Suburban, and so on, celebrated the triumphs of James R. Keene and his racing cohorts and other famous stable-owners on near-by courses. A famous picture of a naked girl in the waves, sold under the name of "September Morn," was perpetuated—at least it was so thought—by a Waldorf cocktail. However, that cocktail was not a brand-new composition —simply a Clover Club cocktail in which Gin gave place to Bacardi Rum; the real Clover Club being composed of the juice of half a Lemon, half a teaspoonful of Sugar, half a pony of Raspberry Syrup, one-quarter pony of White of Egg, and a jigger of Gin.

The Spanish-American War produced distinctive drink nomenclature. The guns of Santiago awakened reverberation in the Waldorf Bar, and shook up what was termed a Santiago Sour—not, however, strictly a cocktail; no more was Hobson's Kiss, reminiscent of an episode that, alas! served to discredit the hero of the *Merrimac*. Then there was a Schley punch, a Shafter cocktail, and another which took its name from Admiral Dewey, victor at Manila Bay.

And when these are named, one has not really begun on the list of appetizers available to those who resorted at regular times to what was long the most famous expositor of the American School of Drinking. As I have said, their nomenclature deserves to live in history, of which it is a part. More, if only to clarify that portion of history with data furnishing contributory evidence—if further proof is impossible—their composition is important to the historian, and some day will so prove to the antiquarian, who will no doubt find material for study and zealous contemplation, if not amazement, in the fact that men once were able, year after year, to get outside so many kinds of more or less ardent spirit, and in such quantity, and still survive.

Well, they didn't all survive. They made patients for the specialists at Carlsbad and other European cure resorts, and in many cases quit this sphere when still in their prime. But when all is said, the searcher for prehistoric man, for ancestors of much greater stature, may halt when he reads of the exploits of the exponents of the old American School of Drinking, point to the record, scratch his head, and say: "There were giants in those days." And others, of course, will draw a moral.

IV. FORMULARY

A.

DRUNK AT THE OLD WALDORF BAR

FOR the convenience of students of the cultural history and *mores* of the American people, as well as for those who wish to set a goal before starting to mix, the bibulous concoctions long known and served at the Bar of the Old Waldorf have been arranged alphabetically, and in two general classes. The cocktails have been set down in one list and the others, which might be classed as "beverages," though that title might be open to dispute, have been termed "Fancy Potations and Otherwise." The latter, as already indicated, have themselves been subdivided into "families" bearing a sort of generic name. However, a great many proved too individualistic to classify, and these are merely run alphabetically.

At the Old Waldorf-Astoria Bar a good many non-alcoholic drinks were made and served, and their recipes are included in a separate list.

For the guidance, particularly, of those faced by bottles of authentic liquors and liquids more or less potent and potable, and who may not know just what to do with them, I have separated names of the cocktails contained in the Old Waldorf Bar Book into lists, governed by the particular "base" on which each was made. Many duplications of names will be discovered, but they are intentional, and due to the fact that some cocktails had more than one base.

In addition is given a list of cocktails in which Vermouth

is used. In a few it formed the base, or one of the bases. Another table names the cocktails in which Absinthe was considered essential. These lists apply only to the cocktails known and served before the Noble Experiment was launched, and not to "Fancy Potations and Otherwise," of the same period, which have been divided, when possible, into groups according to their general name, such as "Slings," "Sours," "Punches," and so on. Further on in the book will be found the best list, with formulas, of worth-while cocktails, punches and so on, such as Americans going to the Tropics and elsewhere abroad have learned to know and usually to esteem, particularly those based upon two of the best known varieties of Rum produced in the West Indies.

LISTS OF PRE-WAR COCKTAILS BY BASES

ON A GIN BASE

Adirondack	Brandy	Cooperstown
Alaska	Bridal	Cornell
Alexander	Brighton	Coxey
All Right	Bronx	Criss Racquet Club
Alphonse	Bronx No. 2	Daniel de Rouge
Ampersand	Original Bronx	Defender
Amsterdam	Bunyan	Delatour
Astor	Chanler	Delmonico
Astoria	Chanticleer	Dewey
Baco	Chauncey	Dr. Cook
Ballantine	Chocolate Soldier	Dorflinger
Bishop Poker	Christ	Dorlando
Black	Clover Club	Dowd
Blackthorn	Club	Down
Bradford	Colonial	Easy

Eddy
Emerson
Fin de Siècle
Fourth Degree
Gibson
Gibson No. 2
Gin
Gladwin
Gold
Good Times
Grand Vin
Guion
Hall
Halsey
Hamlin
Hearst
Hilliard
Holland Gin
Honolulu
Honolulu No. 3
Howard
Ideal
I. D. K.
I. D. K. No. 2
James
Jazz
Jimmie Lee
Jitney
Jockey Club
Johnson
Lewis
Lone Tree
Love
Lynne
MacLean

Marble Hill
Marguerite
Marmalade
Martini
Dry Martini
Middleton
Milliken
Millionaire
Milo
Montauk
Mrs. Thompson
My Own
Newman
Newport
Number Three
Nutting
Oliver
Opal
Orange Blossom
Orange Blossom
   No. 2
Passipe
Pell
Perfect
Perfect No. 2
Poet's Dream
Pomeroy
Porto Rico
Prince Henry
Princeton
Queen
Racquet Club
Rees
Rose
Rossington

Rossington No. 2
St. Francis
St. John
St. Peter
Shafter
Shake-up-Silo
Silver
Sir Jasper
Skipper
Sloe Gin
Somerset
Soul Kiss
Sunshine
Swan
Tango
Thanksgiving
Third Degree
Three-to-One
Tom Gin
Trilby
Turf
Tuxedo
Union League
Vandervere
Van Wyck
Wall Street
Walter Monteith
West India
White Elephant
H. P. Whitney
Widow
Wild Cherry
Yale
Zaza
1915

ON A WHISKEY BASE

(B. indicates Bourbon; S., Scotch; I., Irish; otherwise Rye was used)

Amaranth
Beadleston
Beadleston No. 2
(S.)
Brown
Chauncey
Commodore No. 2
(B.)
Emerald (I.)
Ewing
Express (S.)
Fanciulli
Gloom Lifter (I.)
Hearn's
Highland (S.)
Honolulu No. 2

Japalac
Liberal
Manhattan
Manhattan Junior
Manhattan Punch
McKinley's Delight
Narragansett
Old Fashioned
Whiskey (B. or
Rye)
Pan American
Prince
Robert Burns (S.)
Robin (S.)
Rob Roy (S.)
Rory O'More (I.)

Rosemary (B.)
Sazerac (B. or S.)
Sherman
Southgate
Suburban
Thompson
Waldorf
Waldorf Gloom
Lifter (I.)
Whiskey (B., S., I.
or Rye)
Whiskey Old Style
(B. or Rye)
York (S.)

ON A BRANDY OR A LIQUEUR BASE

(B. indicates Brandy. See also "Drinks from Other Climes")

Alaska (Chartreuse)
Alexander (Crème
de Cacao)
Alphonse (Crème de
Cacao)
Ampersand (B.)
Bijou (Grand Mar-
nier)
Bird (B. and Cura-
çao)
Brandy (B.)
Brandy Crusta (B.)
Brant (B. & White
Mint)

Charlie Rose (B.)
Chauncey (B.)
Chocolate
(Chartreuse and
Maraschino)
Coffee (B.)
Commodore No. 2
(Crème de Cacao)
Coronation
(Apricot Brandy)
Fanciulli (Fernet
Branca)
Floater (B. and
Kümmel)

Full House
(Chartreuse and
Benedictine)
Goat's Delight
(B. and Kirsch-
wasser)
Harvard (B.)
Honolulu No. 3
(Curaçao)
Hop Frog (B.)
Hop Toad (Apricot
Brandy)
Jack Rose (Grena-
dine)

Japanese (B.)
Metropole (B.)
Middleton (Grena-
    dine)
Montana (B.)
Netherland
    (B. and Curaçao)
Peacock (B.)
Peplo (7 Bases, q.v.)
Poet's Dream
    (Benedictine)

Rose (Grand Mar-
    nier)
Ruby (Cherry
    Brandy)
Russian (B.)
Sam Ward (Char-
    treuse)
Skipper (Maraschi-
    no)
Stephen's
    (Benedictine)

Strawberry (B.)
Tango No. 2 (Bene-
    dictine)
Three-to-One
    (Apricot Brandy)
Waldorf-Astoria
    (Benedictine)
Woxum (Char-
    treuse)
"1915" (Curaçao)

ON A RUM BASE

(For many other Rum Cocktails, see "Drinks from Other Climes")

Bacardi
Bacardi No. 2
Commodore
Cora Middleton
Hop Toad

Middleton
Palmetto
Peg o' My Heart
Polo
Raleigh

Santiago
September Morn
Suburban
Tango No. 2

ON A SLOE GIN BASE

Arctic
Ardsley
Bradford
Charlie Chaplin

Futurity
Ping Pong
Porto Rico
Sloe Gin

Tipperary
Tyrone
Van Wyck

ON A BASE OF APPLE WHISKEY, APPLE BRANDY, APPLEJACK, OR "JERSEY LIGHTNING"

Coronation (Applejack)
Full House (Apple Whiskey)
Jack Rose (Applejack)
Jersey (Apple Whiskey)

Marconi Wireless (Applejack)
Normandie (Apple Whiskey)
Star (Apple Whiskey)

IN WHICH IS CALISAYA

Arctic	Colonial	Riding Club
Ardsley	Daniel de Rouge	Robin
Brut	Dorando	
Calisaya	James	

WITH DUBONNET

Chocolate Soldier	Merry Widow	Zaza
Marble Hill	Salomé	

WITH SHERRY

Adonis	Bamboo	Tuxedo
Armour	Stephen's	

WITH PORT

Coffee	Suburban	Union League

WITH SWEDISH PUNSCH

Astor	Doctor

COCKTAILS IN WHICH ABSINTHE IS USED

Absinthe	Goat's Delight	Russian
Ballantine	Hearn's	Salomé
Brut	Loftus	Sazerac
Creole	McKinley's Delight	Sherman
Crook	Opal	Swan
Dorflinger	Peacock	Third Degree
Duchess	Pick-Me-Up	Vivary
Duke	Rees	Waldorf
Fourth Degree	Robert Burns	

IN WHICH VERMOUTH IS USED

Adonis	Defender	Ideal
All Right	Delatour	I. D. K.
Ampersand	Delmonico	I. D. K. No. 2
Amsterdam	Dewey	Japalac
Armour	Dowd	Jazz
Astoria	Down	Jimmie Lee
Baco	Duchess	Johnson
Ballantine	Duke	Lewis
Bamboo	Duplex	Liberal
Beadleston	Easy	Lieut. Colonel
Beadleston No. 2	Eddy	Loftus
Bijou	Emerald	Lone Tree
Bishop Poker	Emerson	Love
Black	Express	Lynne
Blackthorn	Fanciulli	MacLean
Bradford	Fin de Siècle	Manhattan
Bridal	Florida	Manhattan Junior
Brighton	Fourth Degree	Manhattan Punch
Bronx	Futurity	Marconi Wireless
Bronx No. 2	Gibson	Marguerite
Original Bronx	Gibson No. 2	Marmalade
Brown	Gladwin	Martini
Brut	Good Times	Dry Martini
Chanler	Gold	McKinley's Delight
Chanticleer	Grand Vin	Merry Widow
Chauncey	Guion	Metropole
Christ	Hall	Metropolitan
Club	Halsey	Milliken
Cooperstown	Hamlin	Millionaire
Cornell	Harvard	Milo
Coronation	Hearn's	Montauk
Coxey	Hearst	Mrs. Thompson
Creole	Highland	My Own
Criss Racquet Club	Hilliard	Narragansett
Crook	Honolulu No. 2	Neudine

Newman
New Orleans
Newport
Normandie
Number Three
Nutting
Olivet
Opal
Orange Blossom
Palmetto
Passipe
Pell
Perfect
Perfect No. 2
Pick-Me-Up
Poet's Dream
Pomeroy
Prince Henry
Queen
Racquet Club
Rees
Robert Burns
Rob Roy

Rory O'More
Rosemary
Rossington
Rossington No. 2
Ruby
St. Francis
St. John
Salomé
Sazerac
Shafter
Shake-up Silo
Sherman
Silver
Sir Jasper
Somerset
Soul Kiss
Star
Stephen's
Sunshine
Swan
Tango
Tango No. 2
Thanksgiving

Third Degree
Thompson
Tipperary
Tip Top
Trilby
Turf
Tyrone
Vandervere
Vermouth (French)
Vermouth (Italian)
Vin Mariani
Vivary
Waldorf
Wall Street
Walter Monteith
West India
White Elephant
H. P. Whitney
Whittaker
Widow
Woxum
Yale
York

COCKTAILS *

GENERAL DIRECTION: The best method of making most cocktails is to put the ingredients into a shaker in the order named in the
recipe; then add cracked ice; then shake vigorously and long; then
strain the contents into the cocktail glass and serve promptly. Certain
recipes, however, call for "stirring." These are marked "(Stir),"
usually on the last line of the formula. Shaking makes a weaker drink.

* Explanation or exposition of names of recipes starred has been
given earlier in the book. No effort has been made to compile an en-
cyclopedia, the author believing that research specialists interested in
American *mores* would appreciate being left a little wet virgin territory of their own.

ABSINTHE   Two dashes of Gin
Two-thirds Absinthe
One-third Water (Stir)

ADIRONDACK   One-half Orange Juice
One-half Gordon Gin
Rugged, like its namesake. So rugged, indeed, it survived through the prohibition stress and, except that
the "gin" might be almost anything else, was one of the
few cocktail recipes widely known and followed in this
country. But most who made it and drank it did not know
its original name!

ADONIS   Two dashes Orange Bitters
One-half Sherry
One-half Italian Vermouth (Stir)
Named in honor of a theatrical offering which first
made Henry E. Dixey and Fanny Ward famous.

ALASKA   Dash of Orange Bitters
One-third Yellow Chartreuse
Two-thirds Tom Gin

ALEXANDER   One-third Gin
One-third Crème de Cacao
One-third Cream

ALL RIGHT   One-fifth Italian Vermouth
Four-fifths Nicholson Gin
Piece of Orange Peel in Glass

ALPHONSE   One-third Crème de Cacao
One-third Dry Gin
One-third Cream (no ice)

A cartoonist created a series of newspaper comics some thirty years ago, based upon traditional French politeness. "After you, my dear Gaston," "After you, my dear Alphonse," was the text or tenor of the captions.

AMARANTH   One dash Angostura Bitters
Two-thirds jigger Whiskey
Stir; fill from siphon; add powdered Sugar

AMMONIA   Five drops Aromatic Spirits Ammonia
One jigger Water (Stir)
Considered a cure, rather than a cause.

AMPERSAND   Two dashes Orange Bitters
One-third Brandy
One-third Tom Gin
One-third Italian Vermouth
Two dashes of Curaçao on top

AMSTERDAM   One-third   Vermouth   (French   or
Italian)
Dash Orange Bitters
Two-thirds Nicholson's Gin (Stir)
Lemon Peel, squeezed on top

ARCTIC *   Dash of Orange Bitters
One-half Red Calisaya Bark
One-half Sloe Gin (Stir)

ARDSLEY   Dash of Orange Bitters
One-half Red Calisaya
One-half Sloe Gin
Residents of a famous and wealthy community up the

Hudson, by that name, furnished a good deal of patronage to the Bar.

ARMOUR * Two dashes Orange Bitters
One-half jigger Sherry
One-half jigger Italian Vermouth (Stir)

ASTOR   One dash of Lemon Juice
One dash of Orange Juice
One jigger of Gin
One jigger of Swedish Punsch (Stir)
  Perhaps after William Waldorf, who built the original Waldorf. However, chances are, it was originated either at the old Astor House or the Astor Hotel, and took its name from its bar of nativity.

ASTORIA Two dashes Orange Bitters
One-third Tom Gin
Two-thirds French Vermouth (Stir)
  After the big annex to the old Waldorf, which at its opening, in 1897, became the main part of the establishment.

BACARDI Two jiggers Bacardi Rum
Two Limes
A little Sugar
A little Grenadine

BACARDI Juice of one Lime
No. 2   One-half spoonful Sugar
A drink of Bacardi Rum
A little Pineapple Juice
Champagne glass, with shaved Ice

BACO   Dash of Orange Bitters
                One-quarter Italian Vermouth
                One-quarter French Vermouth
                One-half Gordon Gin (Stir)
                Slice of Orange Peel, whiskey glass

BALLANTINE   Two dashes Orange Bitters
                One-half jigger French Vermouth
                One-half jigger Plymouth Gin
                One dash Absinthe

BAMBOO   Two dashes Orange Bitters
                One-half Sherry
                One-half French Vermouth (Stir)

BEADLESTON * Two dashes Orange Bitters
                One-half jigger French Vermouth
                One-half jigger Whiskey (Stir)

BEADLESTON   One-half French Vermouth
No. 2 *   One-half Haig & Haig Scotch Whiskey

BIJOU   Two dashes Orange Bitters
                One-half French Vermouth
                One-half Grand Marnier (Stir)

BIRD   Twist two pieces Orange Peel
                Fill glass with fine Ice
                Two-thirds Triple Sec Curaçao
                One-third Brandy
                Two more Twisted Orange Peels
                Serve as Crème de Menthe Frappé
         So named by the person on whom it was first tried.
   "That's a bird!" he exclaimed, smacking his lips.

BISHOP   One-third French Vermouth
POKER   One-third Italian Vermouth
One-third Plymouth Gin
Dash of Amer Picon Bitters

BLACK   Two-thirds Italian Vermouth
One-third Tom Gin

BLACK-   One pony Kirschwasser
JACK   One dash Brandy
One pony Coffee (claret glass)
Supposed to have been called that from knockout ef-
fects consequent upon indulgence.

BLACK-   Two dashes Orange Bitters
THORN   One-third Italian Vermouth
Two-thirds Sloe Gin (Stir)
Sloe Gin, a distillation of the fruit of the blackthorn,
gave authority to the drink and to its derivation as well.

BRADFORD   Two dashes Orange Bitters
One-half Italian Vermouth
One-half Tom Gin
Twist Lemon Peel on top

BRANDY   One dash Angostura Bitters
One dash Gin
One jigger Brandy (Stir)

BRANDY   One-half Brandy or Applejack
No. 2   One-half French Vermouth
One dash Orange Bitters

BRANDY   Cup one-half small Lemon
CRUSTA   Put in cocktail glass
            Dip edge of glass in powdered Sugar
            In mixing glass put two dashes Angostura
              Bitters
            Four drops Lemon Juice
            Two dashes Curaçao
            Jigger Brandy (Stir and pour)

BRANT   Two dashes Angostura Bitters
            One-quarter White Mint
            Three-quarters Brandy (Stir)
            Piece of Lemon Peel on top

BRIDAL   Two dashes Orange Bitters
            Dash of Maraschino
            One-third jigger Italian Vermouth
            Two-thirds jigger Plymouth Gin (Stir)
            Piece of Orange Peel, twisted, in glass

BRIGHTON Dash of Orange Bitters
            One-half Tom Gin
            One-half Italian Vermouth (Stir)
        So called from the race course near Brighton Beach,
    where many Bar habitués spent their afternoons when
    that track topped the racing calendar.

BRONX   One-fourth Italian Vermouth
            One-fourth French Vermouth
            One-half Gordon Gin
            Piece of Orange Peel

BRONX	Two jiggers Gin
No. 2	One jigger French Vermouth
	One-half jigger Orange Juice

BRONX	Two-thirds Gin
(WAL-	One-third Orange Juice
DORF)	Two slices fresh Pineapple in glass

BRONX	One-third Orange Juice
(Original)	Two-thirds Gin
	Dash of French Vermouth
	Dash of Italian Vermouth

Many claimants to the honor of inventing the Bronx have arisen. It was an Old Waldorf tradition that the inventor was Johnnie Solon (or Solan), popular as one of the best mixers behind its bar counter for most of the latter's history. This is Solon's own story of the Creation—of the Bronx:

"We had a cocktail in those days called the Duplex, which had a pretty fair demand. One day, I was making one for a customer when in came Traverson, head waiter of the Empire Room—the main dining room in the original Waldorf. A Duplex was composed of equal parts of French and Italian Vermouth, shaken up with squeezed orange peel, or two dashes of Orange Bitters. Traverson said, 'Why don't you get up a new cocktail? I have a customer who says you can't do it.'

" 'Can't I?' I replied.

"Well, I finished the Duplex I was making, and a thought came to me. I poured into a mixing glass the equivalent of two jiggers of Gordon Gin. Then I filled the jigger with orange juice, so that it made one-third of orange juice and two-thirds of Gin. Then into the mixture I put a dash each of Italian and French Vermouth, shaking the thing up. I didn't taste it myself, but I poured it into a cocktail glass and handed it to Traverson and said: 'You are a pretty good judge. (He was.) See what you think of that.' Traverson tasted it. Then he swallowed it whole.

" 'By God!' he said, 'you've really got something new! That will make a big hit. Make me another and I will take it back to that customer in the dining room. Bet you'll sell a lot of them. Have you got plenty of oranges? If you haven't, you better stock up, because I'm going to sell a lot of those cocktails during lunch.'

"The demand for Bronx cocktails started that day. Pretty soon we were using a whole case of oranges a day. And then several cases.

"The name? No, it wasn't really named directly after the borough or the river so-called. I had been at the Bronx Zoo a day or two before, and I saw, of course, a lot of beasts I had never known. Customers used to tell me of the strange animals they saw after a lot of mixed drinks. So when Traverson said to me, as he started to take the drink in to the customer, 'What'll I tell him is the name of this drink?' I thought of those animals, and said: 'Oh, you can tell him it is a "Bronx." ' "

BROWN   Two dashes Orange Bitters
         One-half French Vermouth
         One-half Whiskey
    Ascribed to students of Brown University, an early Rockefeller Center.

BRUT Two dashes Orange Bitters
One-half French Vermouth
One-half Calisaya
One dash Absinthe

An extremely "dry" cocktail. "Brut" (French) means "raw." Many customers pronounced it "Brute," and so thought it.

BUNYAN * Gordon Gin
One Olive
Carbonic on side

CALISAYA Two dashes Orange Bitters
One jigger Calisaya (Stir)

CHAMPAGNE One lump Sugar
Two dashes Angostura Bitters
One piece Lemon Peel, twisted
Fill glass with chilled Champagne

CHANLER One small piece of Ice in mixing glass
Squeeze one piece of Lemon Peel
One-third Italian Vermouth
Two-thirds Old Tom Gin (whiskey glass)

"Sheriff Bob" Chanler, artist, married Lina Cavalieri, of the Metropolitan and made the front pages early in the century.

CHANTICLEER One-half Orange Gin
One-half French Vermouth
White of one Egg
(Add a Cock's Comb if desired)

Celebrated the local opening of Edmond Rostand's *Chanticler*.

CHARLIE   One-third Lime Juice
CHAPLIN   One-third Sloe Gin
                 One-third Apricot Brandy

CHARLIE   One pony Brandy
ROSE   Slice of Lemon placed on top (no Ice)

CHAUNCEY *   Dash of Orange Bitters
                 One-fourth Tom Gin
                 One-fourth Whiskey
                 One-fourth Italian Vermouth
                 One-fourth Brandy (Stir)

CHOCOLATE   One pony yellow Chartreuse
                 One pony Maraschino
                 Yolk of one Egg (claret glass)

CHOCOLATE   One-third Dubonnet
SOLDIER *   Two-thirds Nicholson's Gin
                 Dash of Lime Juice

CHRIST   Two dashes Orange Bitters
                 One-half Plymouth Gin
                 One-half Italian Vermouth
                 Two slices Orange Peel

CIDER   Two dashes Angostura Bitters
                 Whole Lemon Peel
                 One lump Ice in Collins glass
                 One pint Cider (Stir)

CLIQUET   Juice one Orange
One jigger Rye; flavored with St.
Croix Rum
One lump Ice (Stir)

CLOVER CLUB   Juice one-half Lemon
One-half spoon Sugar
One-half pony Raspberry Syrup
One-fourth pony White of Egg
One jigger Gin (star glass)
A Philadelphia importation, originated in the bar of
the old Bellevue-Stratford, where the Clover Club,
composed of literary, legal, financial and business lights
of the Quaker City, often dined and wined, and wined
again.

CLUB   Dash of Angostura Bitters
One-third Italian Vermouth
Two-thirds Plymouth Gin (Stir)

COFFEE   Two ponies Port Wine
One pony Brandy
Yolk of one Egg
One-half spoon Sugar (claret glass)

COLONIAL   Dash of Orange Bitters
Two-thirds Plymouth Gin
One-third Red Calisaya (Stir)

COMMODORE   One-half teaspoon Sugar
One dash Lemon Juice
White of one Egg
One drink of Bacardi Rum

One dash of Grenadine
One dash of Raspberry Syrup

COMMODORE   One-third Lemon Juice
No. 2   One-third Bourbon Whiskey
One-third Crème de Cacao
Dash Grenadine Syrup (champagne
glass)

COOPERSTOWN   Bronx, with fresh Mint

CORA   Clover Club made with Jamaica
MIDDLETON   Rum instead of Gin (claret glass)

CORNELL   One-half French Vermouth
One-half Gordon Gin
A compliment to an institution at Ithaca, many of
whose alumni—mining engineers and others—used it to
toast Alma Mater.

CORONATION *   One-third Italian Vermouth
One-third French Vermouth
One-third Applejack
One dash Apricot Brandy

COXEY *   Dash of Amer Picon Bitters
One-half Italian Vermouth
One-half Plymouth Gin (Stir)

CREOLE   Dash of Orange Bitters
One-third jigger Absinthe
One-third jigger Italian Vermouth

CRISS   Dash of Orange Bitters
RACQUET CLUB   One-half French Vermouth

One-half Plymouth Gin
Frappé with Orange Peel

CROOK   Dash of Orange Bitters
One-third Absinthe
Two-thirds Italian Vermouth

DANIEL   Orange Bitters
De ROUGE   One-half Tom Gin
One-half Red Calisaya (Stir)

DEFENDER   Dash of Orange Bitters
One-half Tom Gin
One-half Italian Vermouth
Two dashes Crème Yvette (Stir)
The name of an American yacht which took care of
one of Sir Thomas Lipton's early but seemingly endless
"Shamrocks."

DELATOUR   One-third Italian Vermouth
Two-thirds Gordon Gin
Two dashes Orange Bitters
Twist Orange Peel in glass

DELMONICO   Dash of Orange Bitters
One-half French Vermouth
One-half Plymouth Gin
Two slices Orange Peel
Adopted from the bar of Old Delmonico's, a long-
famous New York restaurant.

DEWEY *   Dash of Orange Bitters
One-half Plymouth Gin
One-half French Vermouth

DOCTOR   One-half Lime Juice
                  One-half Swedish Punsch

DR. COOK *   Juice one-half Lemon
                  White of one Egg
                  Two dashes Maraschino
                  Three-fourths Gin (claret glass)

DORFLINGER *   Dash of Orange Bitters
                  One-third Green Absinthe
                  Two-thirds Plymouth Gin

DORLANDO   Same as Daniel de Rouge
   After an Italian marathon runner in the Olympic
games in London, 1908.

DOWD   One-half Italian Vermouth
                  One-half Gordon Gin

DOWN   Dash of Orange Bitters
                  One-third Italian Vermouth
                  Two-thirds Gordon Gin (with
                      Olive)
   What else, in faith, than a county in Ireland—ancient
home of many American bartenders?

DUCHESS   Dash of Orange Bitters
                  One-third Absinthe
                  One-third French Vermouth
                  One-third Italian Vermouth

DUKE   Dash of Orange Bitters
                  Two dashes, each of Absinthe and
                      Anisette
                  One jigger French Vermouth

DUPLEX   Two dashes Orange Bitters, or two
              squeezes of Orange Peel
              One-half Italian Vermouth
              One-half French Vermouth

EASY   Dash of Orange Bitters
              One-eighth Italian Vermouth
              Seven-eighths Booth's Gin

EDDY *   One-third Gordon Gin
              One-third French Vermouth
              One-third Orange Juice

EMERALD   Dash of Orange Bitters
              One-half Italian Vermouth
              One-half Irish Whiskey (Stir)

EMERSON   Juice one-half Lime
              Small teaspoon Maraschino
              One-third Italian Vermouth
              One-third Tom Gin (Stir)

EWING   One drop Angostura Bitters
              One jigger Whiskey (Stir)

EXPRESS   Dash of Orange Bitters
              One-half Italian Vermouth
              One-half Scotch Whiskey (Stir)

FANCIULLI   One-fourth Fernet Branca
              One-fourth Italian Vermouth
              One-half Whiskey
              Frappé or not. Devotees usually took
              it without Ice.

FIN DE SIÈCLE *   Orange Bitters
                   One dash Amer Picon Bitters
                   One-third Italian Vermouth
                   Two-thirds Plymouth Gin (Stir)

FLOATER   Fill glass with shaved Ice
                   Three-fourths Gilka Kümmel
                   One-fourth Brandy
There is equal authority for a contention that this was
called after a racehorse owned by the late James R.
Keene, or after an individual numerically important,
and who was transported into various precincts at different hours of Election Day and thereby enabled to
vote early and often, as the saying was.

FLORIDA   One-half Italian Vermouth
                   One-half Orange Juice

FOURTH DEGREE One-third Italian Vermouth
                   Two-thirds Plymouth Gin
                   Dash of Absinthe

FULL HOUSE   Dash of Angostura Bitters
                   One-third Yellow Chartreuse
                   One-third Benedictine
                   One-third Apple Whiskey
The name is indicative of the sway once enjoyed by
what was the great American indoor game in B.C. days
—that is to say Before Contract, or Before Culbertson.

FUTURITY *   Dash of Angostura Bitters
                   One-half Sloe Gin
                   One-half Italian Vermouth (Stir)

GIBSON

One-half French Vermouth
One-half Dry Tom Gin (Stir)
Squeeze Lemon Peel on top

GIBSON No. 2

One-third French Vermouth
Two-thirds Plymouth Gin
Orange Peel on top

GIN

Dash of Orange Bitters
One jigger Tom Gin (Stir)

GINGER ALE

One lump Ice
Two dashes Angostura Bitters
One whole Lemon Peel
Fill with cold Ginger Ale

GLADWIN

Three-fourths Gordon Gin
One-eighth Italian Vermouth
One-eighth French Vermouth

GLOOM LIFTER

Same as Clover Club
Irish Whiskey instead of Gin
One-half teaspoon Brandy

GOAT'S DELIGHT

One-half Kirschwasser
One-half Brandy
One dash Orgeat Syrup
One spoon Cream
One dash Absinthe

As to who was the original "goat" cheered by this cup, records are at least vague.

GOLD

Dash of Orange Bitters
One-half Tom Gin
One-half Italian Vermouth

After the product of "them thar hills," finders of which came to the Bar in great numbers.

GOOD TIMES *   Dash of Orange Bitters
One-third French Vermouth
Two-thirds Booth's Gin (Stir; Olive)

GRAND VIN   One-fourth Italian Vermouth
One-fourth French Vermouth
One-half Plymouth Gin

GUION   Dash of Orange Bitters
One-half Plymouth Gin
One-half Italian Vermouth
One spoon of Benedictine on top

Called after a member of the family which owned, or had founded, the Guion line of steamships.

HALL   Dash of Orange Bitters
One-third jigger Italian Vermouth
One-third French Vermouth
One-third Nicholson Gin (Olive)

HALSEY   One-half Gordon Gin
One-fourth Italian Vermouth
One-fourth French Vermouth
Squeeze Orange Peel (whiskey glass)

Named in compliment to a well known stock-broker and patron of the Bar.

HAMLIN   One-third Italian Vermouth
Two-thirds Nicholson Gin

Took its name from Harry Hamlin of Buffalo, an

enthusiastic automobilist in the days when there were
far more enthusiasts than automobiles.

HARVARD   Dash of Orange Bitters
Two-fifths jigger Brandy
Three-fifths Italian Vermouth (Stir)
Fill from chilled siphon
Named after a school for young men, whose site is
contiguous to the Charles River, in a suburb of Boston.
Alumni who drank it sometimes lost the "Harvard
accent."

HEARN'S   Dash of Manhattan Bitters
One-third Whiskey
One-third Italian Vermouth
One-third Absinthe

HEARST *   One dash Orange Bitters
One dash Angostura Bitters
One-half jigger Italian Vermouth
One-half jigger Plymouth Gin

HIGHLAND   Dash of Orange Bitters
One-half Scotch
One-half Italian Vermouth (Stir)

HILLIARD   Dash of Peychaud Bitters
One-third Italian Vermouth
Two-thirds Dry Gin (Stir)

HOFFMAN   Two dashes Orange Bitters
HOUSE   One-third French Vermouth
Two-thirds Plymouth Gin
Squeeze Lemon Peel on top

Conceived at the old Hotel in Madison Square whose bar was famous before the Old Waldorf was built, for the length of its brass rail, the Bougereau painting of nudities on the wall, and the notability of many of its patrons. Served at Old Waldorf Bar, but was not in the original Bar Book.

HOLLAND GIN	Dash of Angostura Bitters One jigger Holland Gin (Stir)
HONOLULU	Two dashes Angostura Bitters One teaspoon Lime Juice One teaspoon Orange Juice One jigger Tom Gin Twist Lemon Peel on top
HONOLULU No. 2	One-third Italian Vermouth One-third French Vermouth One third Whiskey
HONOLULU No. 3	Two jiggers Gin A little less than half a jigger of Orange Curaçao Juice of half a Lime
HOP FROG	Two-thirds Lime Juice One-third Brandy
HOP TOAD	Juice of one-half Lime One-third Jamaica Rum One-third Apricot Brandy
HOWARD	Dash of Orange Bitters One jigger Plymouth Gin (Stir) Two dashes Angostura Bitters

IDEAL One-third Italian Vermouth
Two-thirds Plymouth Gin
Flavor with Grapefruit

I. D. K. One-third Italian Vermouth
Two-thirds Nicholson Gin
Orange Peel (Stir. Bar glass)

I. D. K. No. 2 One-fifth Italian Vermouth
Four-fifths Nicholson Gin
Sprig of Mint

JACK ROSE Juice of Lime
(*or Jacque Rose*) One-third Grenadine Syrup
Two-thirds Applejack
So called because of its pink color, the exact shade of
a Jacqueminot rose, when properly concocted.

JAMES Dash of Orange Bitters
Two-thirds Plymouth Gin
One-third Red Calisaya (Stir)

JAPALAC Juice one-fourth Orange
One jigger French Vermouth
One jigger Whiskey
Dash of Raspberry Syrup
So styled in compliment to a salesman who sold a
product of that name; not because it would enamel a
digestive apparatus.

JAPANESE Dash of Boker's Bitters
Two dashes Orgeat Syrup
One jigger Brandy
One slice Lemon Peel (Stir)

JAZZ   Same as Bronx, with plenty of
                    Orange Juice
    Commemorating the sudden but widespread popu-
larity of modern rhythmical measures when the century
was still young.

JERSEY   Dash of Boker's Bitters
                    Two dashes Syrup
                    One jigger Apple Whiskey (Stir)

JIMMIE LEE   Dash of Peychaud Bitters
                    One-third French Vermouth
                    One-third Italian Vermouth
                    One-third Plymouth Gin
                    Serve with Orange Peel

JITNEY *   One-half Gin
                    One-quarter Lemon Juice
                    One-fourth Orange Juice
                    A little Sugar

JOCKEY CLUB   Dash of Orange Bitters
                    One jigger Dry Gin (Stir)
    Not after the perfume, but after the American Jockey
Club itself.

JOHNSON   Dash of Orange Bitters
                    One-third jigger Plymouth Gin
                    One-third jigger French Vermouth
                    One-third jigger Italian Vermouth
                        (Stir)
                    Piece of Orange Peel on top

LEWIS   One-half French Vermouth
                    One-half Plymouth Gin

Named, not after Sinclair, but before the author of "Main Street" had discovered Broadway.

LIBERAL Dash of Orange Bitters
Three dashes Amer Picon
One-half Whiskey
One-half Italian Vermouth (Stir)

LIEUTENANT One-half French Vermouth
COLONEL One-half Amer Picon Bitters

LOFTUS One-third French Vermouth
One-third Italian Vermouth
One-third Absinthe

Called in compliment to Cissie Loftus, famous English comedienne and mimic, long a popular top-liner.

LONE TREE Dash of Orange Bitters
One-half Italian Vermouth
One-half Plymouth Gin

After the 1899 equivalent of a "nineteenth hole"—a tree which stood alone in a secluded part of a golf course near Philadelphia. Players on that course frequented the Old Waldorf Bar.

LOVE Martini Cocktail, with White of one
Egg added

LYNNE One-half French Vermouth
One-half Gordon Gin

MacLEAN One-quarter Italian Vermouth
One-quarter French Vermouth
One-half Gordon Gin

In honor of John R. MacLean, long proprietor of the Cincinnati *Enquirer* and the Washington *Post*.

McKINLEY'S DELIGHT	One dash Absinthe Two dashes Cherry Brandy Two-thirds Whiskey One-third Italian Vermouth (Stir)

MANHATTAN   Dash of Orange Bitters
One-half Italian Vermouth
One-half Rye Whiskey (Stir)
Serve with Maraschino Cherry

Origin somewhat obscure. Probably first called after a well known club of that name, and not after an island famed for many years as the abode and domain of a certain "Tiger."

MANHATTAN   Two dashes Orange Bitters
No. 2   Two pinches Sugar
One-half Italian Vermouth
One-half Irish Whiskey

MANHATTAN   One-half Vermouth
JUNIOR   One-half Whiskey
Piece of Orange Peel

MANHATTAN   Manhattan cocktail in red ground
PUNCH   glass.—*Editor's Note: Last three*
(Waldorf)   *words denote a container, not an*
ingredient.

MARBLE HILL   One-quarter Dubonnet
One-quarter Orange Juice
One-half Gordon Gin

MARCONI   Two dashes Orange Bitters
WIRELESS *   One-third Italian Vermouth
             Two-thirds Applejack

MARGUERITE   Dash of Orange Bitters
             One-half French Vermouth
             One-half Plymouth Gin

MARMALADE   One-quarter French Vermouth
             One-quarter Italian Vermouth
             One-half Nicholson Gin
             Two slices Orange

MARTINI   Dash of Orange Bitters
             One-half Tom Gin
             One-half Italian Vermouth (Stir)
             Serve with a green Olive
             Twist piece of Lemon Peel on top

MARTINI No. 2   Two jiggers Gin
             One-half jigger Italian Vermouth
             One-half jigger French Vermouth
               (Stir)
             Serve as above

MARTINI (Dry)   Two-thirds Gin
             One-third French (or Sec) Vermouth
               (Stir)
             Serve as above

MARTINI   One-half Gin (preferably dry)
(Dry No. 2) One-half French Vermouth (Stir)
             Serve as above
Modern practice prescribes shaking for a Dry Martini.

This, however, weakens the mixture and used to be discountenanced by barmen who believed in tradition.

MERRY WIDOW *   One-half French Vermouth
One-half Dubonnet

METROPOLE   One dash Peychaud Bitters
One dash Orange Bitters
One-half French Vermouth
One-half Brandy (Stir; Maraschino Cherry)

Attributed to a once well known and somewhat lively hotel, whose bar was long a center of life after dark in the Times Square district.

METROPOLITAN   Two-thirds Manhattan Bitters
One-third Italian Vermouth (Stir)

After a New York club, long popularly called "The Millionaires'."

MIDDLETON   One-half Jamaica Rum
One-quarter Grenadine Syrup
One-quarter Holland Gin
One White of Egg
Juice of one Lemon

MILLIKEN   Three dashes Amer Picon Bitters
One-quarter French Vermouth
One-quarter Italian Vermouth
One-half Gordon Gin

MILLIONAIRE   Dry Martini, with Grenadine on top

MILO   One-sixth Pomelo Bitters
One-third Italian Vermouth

One-half Plymouth Gin

MONAHAN   Dash of Amer Picon Bitters
SPECIAL   Two-thirds Whiskey
                       One-third Italian Vermouth (Stir)
Called after Mike Monahan, one of the Waldorf bar-keepers, its inventor.

MONTANA   One-third Brandy
                       One-third French Vermouth
                       One-third Port Wine (Stir)
A compliment to the field of operations of many early patrons of the Bar.

MONTAUK   One-third French Vermouth
                       One-third Italian Vermouth
                       One-third Gin
                       Two dashes Peychaud Bitters (Stir)
                       Serve in "old-fashioned" glass
Named about the time that men of vision began to talk of Montauk Point as the Western terminus of trans-atlantic steamship lines.

MOUNTAIN   Whiskey glass two-thirds full of Cider
                       One whole Egg
                       Pepper and Salt to taste

MRS. THOMPSON   One-third French Vermouth
                       Two-thirds Gordon Gin

MY OWN   One-half French Vermouth
                       One-half Plymouth Gin

NARRAGANSETT   One-third Italian Vermouth
Two-thirds Rye Whiskey
One dash Anisette (Stir)
After Narragansett Pier, during the "Nineties" the summer abode of many wealthy patrons of the Old Waldorf Bar.

NETHERLAND   Dash of Orange Bitters
Two-thirds Brandy
One-third Curaçao (Stir)
Possibly invented at the Hotel Netherland, a contemporary of the Old Waldorf.

NEUDINE   Dash of Orange Bitters
One-half Italian Vermouth
One-half French Vermouth (Stir)

NEWMAN   Dash of Amer Picon Bitters
One-third French Vermouth
One-third Italian Vermouth
One-third Plymouth Gin
Patronymic of a man who for a time ran the old Haymarket, a widely famed Tenderloin resort.

NEW ORLEANS   Dash of Orange Bitters
One jigger Italian Vermouth
Shake; fizz glass; fill from siphon

NEWPORT   One-fifth Italian Vermouth
Two-fifths French Vermouth
Two-fifths Gordon Gin
Orange Peel

NORMANDIE   Dash of Orange Bitters

One-half jigger Apple Whiskey
One-half Italian Vermouth (Stir)
The name of a hotel in Broadway's early spotlight
district, patronized by sportsmen and sports.

NUMBER THREE   One dash Orange Bitters
One dash Anisette
One-quarter French Vermouth
Three-quarters Nicholson Gin
Squeeze Lemon Peel on top

NUTTING   Dash of Orange Bitters
One-half French Vermouth
One-half Plymouth Gin (Stir)
    Its namesake was Col. Andrew J. Nutting, of Brook-
lyn, an ardent patron of the Bar for many years.

OJEN   One teaspoon Peychaud Bitters
One jigger Ojen
Serve in claret glass with Seltzer

OLD-FASHIONED One-quarter lump Sugar
WHISKEY   Two spoons Water
One dash Angostura
One jigger Whiskey
One piece Lemon Peel
One lump Ice
Serve with small spoon
    This was brought to the Old Waldorf in the days of
its "sit-down" Bar, and was introduced by, or in honor
of, Col. James E. Pepper, of Kentucky, proprietor of a
celebrated whiskey of the period. It was said to have
been the invention of a bartender at the famous Penden-

nis Club in Louisville, of which Col. Pepper was a member.

OLIVET

Dash of Orange Bitters
One-half Tom Gin
One-half Italian Vermouth
Stir; one Olive in glass

OPAL

Dash of Orange Bitters
One-half Plymouth Gin
One-half French Vermouth
Stir; one dash of Absinthe on top

ORANGE
BLOSSOM

One-third Orange Juice
One-third Tom Gin
One-third Italian Vermouth

May have been named by a youthful bartender with romantic spring notions, though the weight of evidence ascribes it to some young bridegroom or other who wanted something novel to use at his final stag party.

ORANGE
BLOSSOM No. 2

One-half Orange Juice
One-half Gin (bar glass)

PALMETTO

Dash of Orange Bitters
One-half St. Croix Rum
One-half Italian Vermouth (Stir)

PAN-AMERICAN

One-half Lemon, muddled
Three dashes Syrup
One jigger Whiskey

PASSIPE

One-third French Vermouth
Two-thirds House of Lords Gin
Juice of one Orange

PEACOCK   Two dashes Amer Picon Bitters
                        One dash Absinthe
                        One jigger Brandy

PEG O'   One-half Lime Juice
MY HEART   One-half Bacardi Rum
                        Color with Grenadine

PELL   One-half Italian Vermouth
                        One-half Nicholson Gin (Olive)

PEPLO   A Pousse Café, shaken and strained
                        (See "Fancy Potations and Other-
                        wise")

PERFECT   One-third Italian Vermouth
                        One-third French Vermouth
                        One-third Plymouth Gin
                        Frappé with an Orange Peel

PERFECT No. 2   One-third Gin
                        One-third Italian Vermouth
                        One-third French Vermouth (Stir)
                        Serve with a green Olive
                        Twist piece of Lemon Peel on top

PICK-ME-UP   Two dashes Acid or Lemon Phos-
                            phate
                        One-half Italian Vermouth
                        One-half Absinthe

PING PONG   Dash of Orange Bitters
                        One-half Sloe Gin
                        One-half French Vermouth

Named after a game said to have originated in England, but which was installed in the big room next to the Old Waldorf Bar in its early days. Bar habitués learned to play it, but sometimes experienced difficulty in hitting the right ball, claiming three or four were going over the net at one time, instead of one.

POET'S DREAM	One-third Benedictine One-third French Vermouth One-third dry Gin Lemon Peel squeezed on top
POLO	One-fourth Lemon Juice One-fourth Orange Juice One-half Rum

Not after Marco, the adventurer, but after the game which, during the "Nineties," was little known except to the fashionable. That was before Meadowbrook had hurled its young men and its wealth into a comparative void in our National outdoor life.

POMEROY	One-third French Vermouth One-third Italian Vermouth One-third Gordon Gin One Orange Peel
PORTO RICO	Sloe Gin Rickey with dash of Grenadine
PRAIRIE (Often called "Prairie Chicken")	One pony Tom Gin One Egg, in claret glass A little Pepper and Salt Cover with Gin Serve with napkin

PRINCE   Two dashes Orange Bitters in
                     glass
                     Whiskey
                     Two dashes Crème de Menthe
                     on top

PRINCE HENRY * Martini, with dash of Crème de
                     Menthe

PRINCETON   Dash of Orange Bitters
                     Two-thirds jigger Tom Gin
                     Stir; fill with Seltzer
   After a college somewhere in New Jersey, which used
to send a lot of young men to the Old Waldorf Bar. Or,
at least, they came.

QUEEN   One-third Italian Vermouth
                     One-third French Vermouth
                     One-third Gin
                     Frappé with fine slice of Pine-
                     apple

RACQUET CLUB * Dash of Orange Bitters
                     One-half Plymouth Gin
                     One-half French Vermouth
                     Orange Peel

RALEIGH   Juice of one-half Lime
                     Juice of one-half Orange
                     Pony of Bacardi Rum
                     Dash of Grenadine Syrup

REES   Wash inside of mixing glass with
                     green Absinthe

One dash Angostura Bitters
One-tenth Italian Vermouth
Nine-tenths Tom Gin (no Ice)

RIDING CLUB *   Dash of Angostura Bitters
One-half pony Acid Phosphate
One jigger Red Calisaya (Stir)

ROBERT BURNS   Dash of Orange Bitters
One dash of Absinthe
One-quarter Italian Vermouth
Three-quarters   Scotch   Whiskey
(Stir)
    It may have been named after the celebrated Scots-
man. Chances are, however, that it was christened in
honor of a cigar salesman, who "bought" in the Old Bar.

ROBIN   One-half Calisaya Bitters
One-half Scotch Whiskey
Stir; serve with a Cherry

ROB ROY *   Dash of Orange Bitters
One-half Scotch
One-half Italian Vermouth
(Stir)

RORY O'MORE   Dash of Angostura Bitters
One-half Irish Whiskey
One-half Italian Vermouth
(Stir)

ROSE   One-fourth Grand Marnier
Three-quarters Dry Gin (Stir)

ROSEMARY *   One-half French Vermouth
                    One-half Bourbon Whiskey

ROSSINGTON   One and one-half jiggers Italian
                        Vermouth
                    Two and one-half jiggers Gor-
                        don Gin
                    Peel of Orange on top

ROSSINGTON No. 2   One-third Dry Gin
                    One-third Italian Vermouth
                    One-third French Vermouth
                    Orange Peel

RUBY   One-third French Vermouth
                    Two-thirds Cherry Brandy
                    Ten drops Acid Phosphate
                    One dash Orange Bitters
                    Two dashes Maraschino

RUSSIAN   Two-thirds Brandy
                    One-third Orange Juice
                    Dash of Orange Bitters
                    Dash of Absinthe

(Another "Russian" contained Vodka, but was seldom
called for.)

ST. FRANCIS *   Two dashes Gordon Orange
                        Bitters
                    One-half Gordon Gin
                    One-half French Vermouth
                    Serve with stuffed Olive

ST. JOHN *   Martini, with dash of Orange
                        Bitters and Lemon Peel
                    (whiskey glass)

ST. PETER *   Juice of two Limes
                One-fourth teaspoon Sugar
                One-half jigger Gordon Gin

SALOMÉ *   Two dashes Absinthe
                One-half Italian Vermouth
                One-half Dubonnet (Stir)

SAM WARD   Cup a small Lemon
                Fill with fine Ice
                Fill with Yellow Chartreuse

SANTIAGO   One-half Orange Juice
                One-half Bacardi Rum
                Color with Grenadine

SAVANNAH   Juice one-half Orange
                Drink of Gin
                White of one Egg (claret glass)
                Dash of Crème de Cacao

SAZERAC   Few dashes of Peychaud Bitters
                Dash of Absinthe
                Dash of Italian Vermouth
                One jigger Bourbon or Scotch

SEPTEMBER   Juice of one Lime
MORN *   One jigger Bacardi Rum
                White of one Egg (claret glass)
                Color with Grenadine

SEPTEMBER   Clover Club; made with Bacardi in-
MORN No. 2   stead of Gin

SHAFTER *   Dash of Orange Bitters

One-half Nicholson Gin
One-half Italian Vermouth (Stir)

SHAKE-UP-SILO One-half French Vermouth
One-half Plymouth Gin

SHERMAN Dash each, Angostura and Orange
Bitters
Three dashes Absinthe
Two-thirds jigger Italian Vermouth
One third jigger Whiskey

SILVER Martini, with dash of Maraschino

SIR JASPER Dash of Orange Bitters
One-third Italian Vermouth
One-third French Vermouth
One-third Tom Gin (Stir)
Twist Lemon Peel on top

SLOE GIN Dash of Orange Bitters
Two-thirds Sloe Gin
One-third Plymouth Gin (Stir)

SODA Two dashes Angostura Bitters
Two lumps Ice (Collins glass)
Two pieces Lemon Peel
One bottle Lemon Soda

SOMERSET One-fourth Italian Vermouth
One-fourth French Vermouth
One-half Tom Gin (Stir)

SOUL KISS One-third French Vermouth
Two-thirds Dry Gin

White of Egg (bar glass)
After a musical comedy of that name, which, because
of its appellation, stirred up a good many ideas among
the young—and middle-aged—about the latter part of
the first decade of the century.

SOUTHGATE   One-fourth lump Sugar dissolved in
one-half pony of Water
Dash of Boonekamp Bitters
One jigger Whiskey
One piece twisted Lemon Peel

STAR   Dash of Orange Bitters
One-half Apple Whiskey
One-half Italian Vermouth (Stir)

STEPHEN'S   One-third Sherry
One-third French Vermouth
One-third Benedictine

STRAWBERRY   Dash of Orange Bitters
Juice of twelve Strawberries, or one
pony of Syrup
Three-quarters Brandy
One dash of Maraschino (Stir)
Strawberry in glass

SUBURBAN *   Dash of Orange Bitters
Dash of Angostura Bitters
One-fifth Port Wine
One-fifth Jamaica Rum
Three-fifths Whiskey

SUNSHINE   Dash of Orange Bitters
One-eighth Italian Vermouth

One-eighth French Vermouth
Three-fourths Tom Gin

SWAN

Juice of one Lime
One-half jigger Swan Gin
One-half jigger French Vermouth
Two dashes Angostura Bitters
Two dashes Absinthe

TANGO

One-half French Vermouth
One-half Dry Gin
White of Egg

After the Argentinian dance which first became popular during the early days of the modern dance craze, in 1912 or 1913.

TANGO No. 2

One-fifth French Vermouth
One-fifth Italian Vermouth
One-fifth Rum
One-fifth Benedictine
One-fifth Orange Juice

THANKSGIVING

No Bitters
One-half Italian Vermouth
One-half Tom Gin
Piece of Orange Peel

THIRD DEGREE *

One-eighth French Vermouth
Seven-eighths Plymouth Gin
Several dashes Absinthe

THOMPSON

One-third Italian Vermouth
Two-thirds Whiskey
One piece each of Orange Peel,
    Pineapple, Lemon Peel

After Denman Thompson, the actor, who made "The
Old Homestead" famous, and upon whom that play had
equally beneficent results.

THREE-TO-ONE   One-half Lime Juice
                 One-third Apricot Brandy
                 Two-thirds Dry Gin

TIPPERARY   Two-thirds Sloe Gin
                 One-third French Vermouth
                 Teaspoon of Lemon Juice
Invented long before the wartime song of that name
was heard, so that it must be considered a direct namesake of an Irish county, and so called by a fond exile.

TIP TOP   Four dashes Benedictine
                 Two dashes Angostura Bitters
                 One jigger French Vermouth (Stir)
                 Serve with Lemon Peel

TOM GIN   Dash of Orange Bitters
                 One jigger Tom Gin (Stir)

TRILBY *   Dash of Orange Bitters
                 One-third French Vermouth
                 Two-thirds Tom Gin
                 One dash of Crème Yvette (Stir)

TURF   Dash of Angostura Bitters
                 One-third Italian Vermouth
                 Two-thirds Holland Gin (Stir)
At times a good half—possibly two-thirds—of the
crowd in the Bar were interested in racing.

TUXEDO Dash of Orange Bitters
Two-thirds Plymouth Gin
One-third Sherry (Stir)
After a settlement on the Erie R. R. where many
customers of the Bar had country places.

TYRONE Dash of Orange Bitters
Two-thirds Sloe Gin
One-third Italian Vermouth (Stir)

UNION Dash of Orange Bitters
LEAGUE * One-third Port Wine
Two-thirds Tom Gin (Stir)

VANDERVERE One-half Nicholson Gin
One-quarter French Vermouth
One-quarter Italian Vermouth (Stir)
Twist Lemon Peel on top

VAN WYCK Dash of Orange Bitters
One-third Sloe Gin
Two-thirds Tom Gin

VERMOUTH Dash of Orange Bitters
(French) One jigger French Vermouth

VERMOUTH Dash of Orange Bitters
(Italian) One jigger Italian Vermouth

VIN MARIANI Dash of Orange Bitters
One-third Italian Vermouth
Two-thirds Vin Mariani

VIVARY Dash of Orange Bitters
One-half Italian Vermouth

One-half French Vermouth
One dash Absinthe

WALDORF   Dash of Manhattan Bitters
                     One-third Whiskey
                     One-third Absinthe
                     One-third Italian Vermouth

WALDORF-   Pony of Benedictine on Ice
ASTORIA   Cover and build mound with sweet-
                     ened Whipped Cream

WALDORF   Juice one-half Lemon
GLOOM-LIFTER   One-half teaspoon Brandy
                     One jigger Irish Whiskey
                     White of one Egg
                     One-half teaspoon Sugar
                     Dash of Raspberry Syrup
                     Dash of Grenadine

WALL STREET   One-third Italian Vermouth
                     Two-thirds Gordon Gin
                     Squeeze of Orange Peel on top

WALTER   One-half Italian Vermouth
MONTEITH   One-half Nicholson Gin

WEST INDIA   Dash of Angostura Bitters
                     One-half Tom Gin
                     One-half French Vermouth (Stir)

WHISKEY   Dash of Angostura Bitters
                     One dash Gin
                     One jigger of Whiskey (Stir)
          See also Old-Fashioned Whiskey.

WHITE   One-third Italian Vermouth
ELEPHANT   Two-thirds Dry Gin
                 White of one Egg

WHITE   Fill lemonade glass two-thirds with
GRAPE-JUICE   Ice and Grape Juice
                 Add Juice of Lime
                 Fill with Seltzer

H. P. WHITNEY   One-quarter Italian Vermouth
                 One-quarter French Vermouth
                 One-half Plymouth Gin
                 Frappé with Orange Peel
A noted patron of the turf who frequented the Bar
before he and his friends moved up to the Brook Club.

WHITTAKER   Dash of Orange Bitters
                 One-third Italian Vermouth
                 Two-thirds Red Calisaya (Stir)

WIDOW   One-half jigger Gordon Gin
                 One-half jigger French Vermouth
                 Juice of an Orange

WILD CHERRY   Dash of Orange Bitters
                 One-half Tom Gin
                 One-half Cherry Brandy (Stir)

WOXUM   One-half pony Yellow Chartreuse
                 One-half jigger Apple Whiskey
                 One-half jigger Italian Vermouth
                     (Stir)
Some think it is aboriginally American, and ascribe

it to a "bunch of Indians," so-called, who occasionally made whoopee—or, as it was said at that time, "raised hell"—in the Old Waldorf Bar when they could get away with it.

YALE   Dash of Orange Bitters
                One-half Tom Gin
                One-half Italian Vermouth (Stir)
                Little Seltzer on top
        An institution somewhere beyond Old Greenwich, where many young men go for the purpose of commuting to New York for week-ends. The Old Bar used to be one of their "ports of call" and there they used to find many who in years past had gone to the same place and done the same things.

YORK   Dash of Orange Bitters
                One-half French Vermouth
                One-half Scotch Whiskey (Stir)

ZAZA *   One dash Orange Bitters
                One-half Plymouth Gin
                One-half Calisaya (Stir)

ZAZA No. 2   Two dashes Orange Bitters
                One-third Tom Gin
                Two-thirds Dubonnet (Stir)

1915   One-third Curaçao
                One-third Cream
                One-third Gin
        Named in honor of a New Year. Some believe this was the last cocktail invented in the Old Waldorf Bar.

FANCY POTATIONS AND OTHERWISE *

Note: The type of serving-glass appears in parenthesis at the end of one line of most formulas.

COBBLERS

COBBLER: A summer drink made of iced wine, sugar, fruit juices, etc. [U.S.]

CLARET   One spoon Sugar
                    Two ponies of Water
                    One and one-half jiggers Claret
                    Fill with Ice; fruit well (goblet)

NARRAGANSETT   Whole peel of Orange
                    Juice of one Orange
                    One jigger Whiskey
                    One bottle Ginger Ale
                    Stir (Collins glass)

SHERRY   One-fourth spoon Sugar
                    One pony of Water
                    One and one-half jigger Sherry
                    Stir; fill with Ice; fruit (goblet)

COOLERS

COOLER: A refreshing beverage—supposed to illustrate its name.

BOSTON   Juice one-half Lemon
                    One-quarter spoon Sugar

* In "Drinks from Other Climes" will be found numerous other classified and miscellaneous mixed drinks.

One jigger Medford Rum
Ice; one bottle plain Soda (Collins glass)

HAWAII

Whole peel of Orange
Juice of one Orange
One jigger Whiskey
Ice; fill Collins glass with Ginger Ale

HILLY CROFT

Whole rind of Lemon
Two lumps Ice
One Ginger Ale
One jigger Tom Gin

KLONDIKE

Whole peel of one Orange
Juice of Orange
One jigger Whiskey
Ice; one Ginger Ale (Collins glass)

REMSEN

Whole peel of Lemon
One jigger Tom Gin
Ice; fill with plain Soda

ROOFGARDEN

One dash Bitters, on one lump Sugar
One jigger French Vermouth
Ice; one bottle of Ginger Ale (Collins)

SEAWANHAKA
YACHT CLUB

Whole peel of one Lemon
Two lumps Ice
One jigger Whiskey
Fill with Ginger Ale (goblet)

CUPS

CUP: A beverage made with wine, generally iced, and with flavoring herbs and fruits. In olden times, vegetables were also included, particularly cucumbers.

CHAMPAGNE (pitcher)
One and one-half ponies Brandy
One pony Benedictine
One pony Maraschino
One bottle Soda
One bottle Wine
One stick Ice
Fruit; decorate with Mint

CLARET CUP WALDORF (pitcher)
One-half spoon Sugar
One and one-half ponies Brandy
Pony each, Benedictine and Maraschino
Seltzer to fill glass
Stir; pour into pitcher; large stick Ice
One bottle Claret
Fruit; decorate with frosted Mint

FRUIT (pitcher)
Equal portions, Raspberry Syrup, Strawberry Syrup, Pineapple Syrup
Lemon and Orange Juice
Currant Syrup
Add Seltzer or Apollinaris to fill
Add sliced Bananas and Strawberries

HOBSON'S KISS
Champagne, Moselle, or Rhine Wine Cup
Made like Claret Cup Waldorf
Commemorating a notable osculation by which enthu-

siastic women, upon his return from Cuban waters, came near dimming the fame of Lieut. Commander Richard Pearson Hobson, U.S.N., who had sunk the collier *Merrimac* in a heroic effort to bottle up the Spanish fleet in Santiago harbor, during the Spanish-American War.

MINEHEART   Equal portions, Raspberry Syrup, Pineapple Juice, Lemon Juice, Orange Juice, Red Currant Juice
Stir; add Ice; fill with Water
Add sliced bananas and whole strawberries

FIZZES

Fizz: An effervescing beverage, named, onomatopoetically, from the noise.

BALTIMORE   One-half pony Anisette
BRACER   One-half pony Brandy
White of one Egg (fizz glass)
Frappé; fizz with Carbonic

BAYARD   One dash Raspberry
BEAUTY   One dash Maraschino
One spoon Lemon Juice
One jigger Tom Gin (lemonade)
Ice; shake; strain; fill with Seltzer

BISMARCK   Juice one-half Lemon
One-half spoon Sugar
One pony Raspberry Syrup
One and one-half jigger Rhine Wine

Shake and strain; fill with chilled
Seltzer

CHICAGO   Juice one-fourth Lemon
One-half spoon Sugar
White of one Egg
One-half jigger Jamaica Rum
One-half jigger Port Wine
Ice; shake; strain; fill from siphon
    An importation from the Windy City long before
bombs, machine guns and sawed-off shotguns had come
to disturb its peaceful life.

FREE SILVER   Juice one-fourth Lemon
One-third spoon Sugar
Two-thirds Tom Gin
One-third Medford Rum
One-half pony of Milk
Ice; shake; strain; fill from siphon
    Free silver was an obsession of a great many Ameri-
cans during the final decade of the last century.

GIN   Juice one-half Lemon
One-half spoon Sugar
One jigger Tom Gin
Shake and strain; fill from chilled
    siphon

GOLDEN   Juice one-half Lemon
One-half spoon Sugar
Yolk one Egg
One jigger Gin
Shake; strain; fill from chilled siphon

GRENADINE   Juice one-half Lemon
One-half spoon Sugar
One pony Grenadine
One pony Milk
One jigger Tom Gin
Ice; shake; strain; fill from siphon

HORTON   Gin fizz, with three or four sprigs
of Mint, shaken up

JAP   Juice one-half Lemon
One spoonful Sugar
One-half jigger each of Rye Whiskey
and Port Wine
White of one Egg
Frappé; strain; serve with Seltzer
and one slice Pineapple

MORNING   Juice one-half Lemon
GLORY   One-half spoon Sugar
White of one Egg
One jigger Scotch
Two dashes Absinthe
Shake; strain; fill from chilled
siphon

MURDOCK   Two lumps Ice, dissolved in pony
of Water
Two pieces Lemon Peel
One jigger Rye Whiskey
Fill glass with Ice
Fizz from siphon

NEW ORLEANS   Juice of one Lemon and a half
              White of Egg
              One spoon Sugar
              Three dashes Orange Water
              One jigger Cream
              One jigger Gin
              Ice; shake well (goblet)

ROYAL   Gin Fizz with a whole Egg (lemon-
              ade)
              Fill from chilled siphon

SILVER   Gin Fizz, with White of Egg
              Fill with Seltzer

STRAWBERRY   One pony Strawberry Syrup
              Juice of one-half Lemon
              One jigger Tom Gin (lemonade)
              Ice; shake; strain; fill from siphon

WHISKEY   Juice of one-half Lemon
              One spoon Sugar
              One jigger Whiskey
              Ice; shake; strain; fill from siphon

WHISKEY   One-half spoon Sugar
No. 2   One-half pony of Water
              Three or four lumps Ice
              One jigger Whiskey
              Three slices of Fruit
              Serve with spoon

FLIPS

FLIP: A drink made with some liquor, mixed with an egg and spiced and sugared.

SHERRY   One Egg (star glass)
                One-half spoon Sugar
                One jigger Sherry
                Ice; shake; strain; grate Nutmeg on
                top
         Note: Other flips made by the same formula, with other bases than Sherry.

KRUGER   Sherry Flip, with a dash of Grenadine
SPECIAL   (fizz glass)
                Fill from siphon

WHISKEY   One Egg
                One-half spoon Sugar
                One jigger Whiskey
                Shake; strain; Nutmeg grated on top

HIGH-BALLS

Just as is the case with "cocktail," the origin and application of "high-ball" as a name for a stimulant is open to discussion. Some have asserted that the name was taken from the National Game, possibly because of the effect upon the "batting average" of one who "hits" enough in rapid succession. However the lexicographer digs further.

In slang, a drink is often described as a "shot"; in Pall-Mall English it's a "spot." High-ball, more or less pure American for what a Britisher calls a Whiskey-and-Soda, say the learned, is combined from "high," meaning tall, and descriptive of the container, and "ball," which used to be the equivalent of "shot," both metallically and absorbatively. Therefore the classical definition, "a 'long' drink consisting of whiskey, to which is added soda-water, mineral water or some other effervescent, served in a tall glass with broken ice."

HIGH-BALL   One jigger Whiskey
One lump Ice
Fill from siphon
    The whiskey might be Scotch, Bourbon, Rye or Irish;
or instead might be used Gin, Sloe Gin, Brandy or Rum,
the particular High-ball taking its name from the liquor
used. In a GINGER ALE HIGH-BALL, Ginger Ale is used
instead of aerated water.

BERMUDA   One-third Brandy
One-third Plymouth Gin
One-third French Vermouth
One whole Lemon Peel
One lump Ice; fill from siphon

PALL MALL   One-third Nicholson Gin
One-third Vermouth
One-third Brandy
Fill from chilled siphon

HOT POTATIONS

COLUMBIA   One-half lump Sugar
SKILL   Two spoons hot Water
One piece twisted Lemon Peel
One jigger Whiskey
Fill with hot Water; small spoon
    Called after the prowess Columbia had exhibited in a
certain boat race with Cornell, and first composed upon
the demand of a Columbia "fan" for a new drink that
would properly commemorate the occasion.

HOT GIN SLING See the same under "SLINGS"

HOT SCOTCH — Lump Sugar, dissolved in hot Water
One jigger Scotch
Fill two-thirds with hot Water
One piece Lemon Peel, twisted

HOT SHERRY — Half lump Sugar, dissolved in hot Water
One jigger Sherry
Fill two-thirds with hot Water
Nutmeg on side

HOT SPICED RUM — Lump Sugar, dissolved in hot Water
One jigger Rum
Five whole Cloves
Fill glass with hot Water

HOT WHISKEY SKIN — Lump Sugar, dissolved in hot Water
One jigger Whiskey
One piece twisted Lemon Peel
Fill with hot Water

LOCOMOTIVE HOT (pitcher) — Yolks of three Eggs, well beaten
One ounce of Honey
Five Cloves
One pony of Triple Sec
One pint Hot Burgundy
Stir well; serve in hot glasses

MULLED CLARET or Burgundy — Three spoons Sugar
One-half pint Water
Five or six Cloves
Three small pieces Cinnamon
Whole rind of Lemon, cut very thin

Let come to a boil; add Wine
Boil again and serve very hot

TOM AND   Beat six Eggs well, adding Pow-
JERRY   dered Sugar until very thick, work-
                 ing out all lumps
                 Pour one-half tablespoon of this
                   batter into mug
                 One-half jigger Brandy
                 One-half jigger Jamaica Rum
                 Fill with hot Water; add Nutmeg
(See also TODDIES, and "Drinks from Other Climes")

HOT—WITH FLAMES

BLUE BLAZES   One lump Sugar dissolved in one-
                 half jigger hot Water (ale mug)
                 One jigger Scotch
                 Set fire to Whiskey; pour back and
                 forth blazing

CAFÉ BRÛLER   Moisten edge of claret glass—dip in
                 Powdered Sugar
                 Seven-eighths Hot Coffee
                 One-eighth Brandy on top
                 Set fire to Brandy

JERSEY   Two lumps Sugar
FLASHLIGHT   One dash Angostura Bitters
                 One piece Lemon Peel
                 One jigger Apple Whiskey
                 Fill with hot Water; ignite the whole
                 Mix while blazing

JULEPS

JULEP: From the Spanish *julepe*, itself derived from the Arabic and Persian *julab* = *gul* (rose) plus *ab* (water); so that the name is of ancient origin. Today, fresh Mint, as part of a julep, is as unchanging as an old-time Persian law.

BRANDY   Put three or four sprigs of Mint in
     mixing glass
     One-half spoon Sugar
     One pony Brandy
     One pony Water; crush well
     Fill goblet two-thirds with Ice
     Strain mixture on top
     Fruit well; decorate with Mint

CHAMPAGNE   One lump Sugar
     Three sprigs Mint
     Two lumps Ice
     Fill with Champagne

MINT   In mixer put three sprigs Mint
     One-half spoon Sugar
     One pony Water
     Press well, crushing Mint
     Add one jigger Whiskey; stir
     Pour into glass two-thirds full Ice
     Fruit well; decorate with Mint

PRESBREY   Three sprigs Mint
     One jigger Whiskey
     One dash St. Croix Rum; shaved
     Ice; stir; Fruit and Mint

WHISKEY MINT   Three sprigs Mint
     One-half spoon Sugar

One pony of Water
Press well and add jigger Whiskey
Ice; stir; strain well

POUSSE CAFÉS

L'AMOUR   One-third Maraschino
Yolk of one Egg
Cover with Vanilla
Fill with Brandy

RAINBOW   Equal parts of Grenadine, Maraschino, Green Crème de Menthe, Yellow Chartreuse, Curaçao and Brandy

WALDORF   One seventh each, Raspberry Syrup, Anisette, Parfait d'Amour, Crème Yvette, Yellow Chartreuse, Green Chartreuse and Brandy (Sherry glass)

PUNCHES

Contrary to common belief, the punch is not exactly an English invention. In its original form the word was the Sanskrit *pancha*, meaning "five." The Hindus used five ingredients to make what they called *panch*—Arrack, tea, sugar, water and lemon. Some attribute its importation into England, not to early British travelers in the Orient, but to the British East India Company, in its efforts to popularize tea. If that looks a bit far-fetched, in modern punches the rule of five ingredients does not always apply.

In addition to the various punches served at the Old Waldorf-Astoria, several scores of others are made in various parts of the world. He or she who complains of lack of "punch" among the drinks listed in this book is advised to consult a standard book of punch recipes.

BOSTON MILK Grate Nutmeg in glass
One-half spoon Sugar
One-half jigger Whiskey
One-half St. Croix Rum (goblet)
Fill with chilled Milk; shake well;
strain

BRANDY   Juice of one-half Lemon
One-half spoon Sugar
One pony of Water
One jigger Brandy
Ice; shake; strain; fruit

CHAMPAGNE   One pint Champagne
(pitcher)   One pint white Beaune, or other white
Wine
One pint Apollinaris
One sliced Orange
Two lumps Sugar; Ice

CHAMPAGNE   One pint Champagne
(KINSLEY)   One pint Burgundy
One pint Apollinaris
Three lumps Sugar
One sliced Orange; Ice

CLARET   Juice one-half Lemon
One-half spoon Sugar
One pony of Water
One and one-half jiggers Claret
Ice; stir; pour into goblet; fruit well

CLARET No. 2 (gallon)	Juice six Lemons Two ponies each, Curaçao and Brandy Tablespoon Sugar Two quarts Claret Ice; two siphons of Seltzer
CREAM	One-half spoon Sugar One pony White Curaçao One pony Brandy Fill two-thirds with chilled Milk Shake well; strain; Nutmeg
CUBAN MILK	One pony Vanilla One-half teaspoon Sugar One whole Egg One pony Bacardi Fill with Milk; shake; strain; Nutmeg
FISH-HOUSE	Juice one-half Lemon One-half spoon Sugar One-half jigger Brandy One-half jigger Jamaica Rum Ice; shake well; fruit in season
GOODWIN	Juice one Lime Open spoon Sugar One dash Sherry One jigger Rye Ice; shake; strain; fruit
HERALD	Juice of one Orange One-half spoon Sugar

One jigger Whiskey
Ice; shake; fruit; flavor with St.
Croix Rum

KNICKERBOCKER   Juice one-half Lemon
One-half spoon Sugar
One pony Water
One jigger St. Croix Rum
Ice; stir; fruit well; float Claret
on top

LANDER'S   One-fourth Jamaica Rum
One-fourth Gordon Gin
One-fourth French Vermouth
One-fourth Lemon Juice; Frappé

MILK   One jigger Whiskey (or Brandy)
One-half spoon Sugar
Fill three-quarters with Milk
Ice; shake; strain; serve with
Nutmeg

PEGGY O'NEILL   One dash Parfait d'Amour
One Lime Peel in center of glass
One drink Rye Whiskey
Three sprigs Mint
Ice; fill with Seltzer

After an opera or play of that name, it is believed.
The original Peggy O'Neill was the daughter of a Washington tavern-keeper, and noted for her beauty and
wit.

PING PONG   Juice of one Lemon
One dash Bitters

One jigger Apple Cider
Fresh Egg
One spoon Sugar
Shake; strain; fill with chilled Soda

PING PONG
No. 2
(pitcher)

Five siphons
One quart Whiskey
One quart Brandy
Crushed Mint; Fruit

PLANTER'S

Juice of one small Lime
Jigger of Jamaica Rum
Fruit like a Claret Punch
Fill glass from chilled siphon

PUNCH
UNIVERSAL

Two tablespoons Sugar
Juice of two Lemons and one
    Orange
One pony Jamaica Rum
One pony Brandy
One bottle plain Soda
One quart Chablis; Ice; Fruit

ROMAN

Juice of one-half Lemon
One spoon Sugar
One pony Curaçao
One-half jigger Jamaica Rum
One-half Brandy
One or two dashes Port Wine
Ice; shake; strain; Seltzer on top;
    Fruit

ROOSEVELT

Muddle one-half Lemon
One spoon Sugar

One jigger Apple Whiskey
Ice; shake; one dash of Brandy on
    top

RUM   Juice of one-half Lemon
                        One-half spoon Sugar
                        One pony of Water
                        One jigger Rum
                        Fill glass two-thirds fine Ice; Fruit

SCHLEY   Juice and rind of one-half Lime
                        One-fourth spoon Sugar
                        One-third jigger St. Croix Rum
                        Two-thirds jigger Whiskey
                        Ice; shake; strain; fill with Seltzer

SHERIDAN   Plain lemonade, with Whiskey
                            on top

STEINWAY   Muddle one-half Lemon
                        One-half spoon Sugar
                        One jigger Whiskey
                        Fill with chilled Seltzer
                        Stir; strain; Fruit
        Named after Charles Steinway, a well-known gour-
met.

WALDORF   Whiskey, with Claret floated on top

WHISKEY   Juice of one-half Lemon
                        One-half spoon Sugar
                        One pony of Water
                        Fill glass two-thirds with fine Ice
                        One jigger Whiskey
                        Stir; fruit well in season

WHISKEY MILK   One-half spoon Sugar
One jigger Whiskey
Fill three-quarters with chilled
Milk
Shake well; strain; Nutmeg on top

RICKEYS

The Rickey owes its name to Colonel "Joe" Rickey, though an interested public has long persisted in referring to him as "Colonel Jim" Rickey. Colonel Rickey had been a lobbyist in Washington, and as such used to buy drinks for members of Congress in the glamorous days before they had come to depend upon the discreet activities of gentlemen in green hats to keep them wet while they voted dry. The drink was invented and named for him at Shoemaker's, famous in Washington as a Congressional hangout.

GIN RICKEY   Juice and rind of one Lime
Lump of Ice (goblet)
Gin to suit customer
Fill from siphon
Note: Other Rickeys get their names from the liquor taking the place of Gin in following the formula.

SANGAREES

The Sangaree probably acquired its name for one or two reasons, or both. The word is derived from the Spanish *sanguia*, meaning "bloody," which itself comes from the Latin *sanguis* (blood), and a sangaree is red, or reddish—or was as originally made. The other reason for the name may be that it is supposed to have a cooling effect upon the blood.

SANGAREE   One-half jigger French Vermouth
One-half jigger Sloe Gin
One dash Acid Phosphate

Two dashes Angostura Bitters
Fill with Ice (fizz glass)

PORT WINE   One-half spoon Sugar
One jigger Water
One and one-half jiggers Port Wine
Ice; stir; strain

Other Sangarees were made similarly of Sherry, or Gin, or Brandy. (See "Drinks from Other Climes.")

SLINGS

SLING: Name, but not the drink itself, ascribed to the German *schlingen*, meaning "swallow," not from the English verb meaning to "hurl"—down.

BRANDY   One-half lump Sugar dissolved in two
spoons Water (whiskey glass)
One jigger Brandy
One piece twisted Lemon Peel
One lump Ice; serve with small spoon

GIN   One lump Sugar, dissolved in half
wine-glass Water
One-half glass Gin
One lump Ice
Stir with spoon; grated Nutmeg

HOT GIN   One lump Sugar, dissolved in hot
Water
One jigger Gin; more hot Water
One piece Lemon Peel

WHISKEY   Half lump Sugar in half pony Water
One jigger Whiskey

Four or five drops Lemon Juice
One piece Lemon Peel; Ice (spoon)

SMASHES

SMASH: To flatten; in tennis, to bat, etc.; in slang a smash is something of extraordinary ability. Somewhere in these lies the origin of the term as "a beverage of spirituous liquors, with mint, water, sugar and ice."

BRANDY   Two sprigs Mint
                Two spoons Water
                One-quarter spoon Sugar
                Muddle in fizz glass
                One jigger Brandy
                Two lumps Ice; serve with small
                spoon

WHISKEY   Three sprigs of Mint
                Fill mixing glass with fine Ice
                Two more sprigs of Mint
                One-quarter spoon Sugar
                One-half pony of Water
                Press well; add one jigger Whiskey
                Stir; strain; fruit well; Mint on top

SOURS

SOUR: A good old Anglo-Saxon word, and it started as *surigan*, was shortened to *sur*, and finally in its more modern version became the name of an alcoholic drink because of the taste of the lemon or lime that is an essential.

BRANDY   Juice one-half Lemon (star glass)
                One-half spoon Sugar

One jigger Brandy
Fill with Ice; stir; strain; fruit

BRUNSWICK   Juice one-half Lemon
One spoon Sugar
One jigger Rye
Ice, Stir; fruit; Claret on top

Invented at the Old Hotel Brunswick, once a resort for Fashion, and situated on the north side of Madison Square.

DOUBLE   Juice one-half Lime
STANDARD   One-half Rye Whiskey
One-half Tom Gin
One dash Raspberry Syrup
Ice; stir; strain; fruit

Owes its name to a controversy which during the Nineties divided two political parties on the subject of whether this country should have both a gold and silver standard of currency, or gold alone. Nothing to do with masculine or feminine conduct.

HANCOCK   Four dashes Rock Candy Syrup
Juice one Lime
Three dashes Jamaica Rum
One jigger Bourbon
Ice; stir; strain; Carbonic (fizz glass)

PEQUOD SOUR   Juice of one-half Lemon
One-half spoon Sugar
Two sprigs Mint
One-half Water

One jigger Whiskey
Stir well; fruit

ROOSEVELT Juice of one-half Lemon
One-half spoon Sugar
One jigger Apple Whiskey
Ice; shake; strain on Fruit in glass
   Nothing to do with the New Deal; named to compliment the author of the Square Ditto.

RUM   Juice of one-half Lemon
One-half spoon Sugar
One jigger Rum
Ice; shake; strain on Fruit in glass

ST. CROIX   Juice of one-half Lemon
One spoon Sugar
One jigger St. Croix Rum
Ice; shake; strain on Fruit in glass

SANTIAGO   Juice of one-half Lemon
One-half spoon Sugar
One pony of Water
One jigger Whiskey
Ice; stir well; stuffed Olive in glass

SOUTHERN   St. Croix Sour, with Claret on top

WHISKEY   Juice of one-half Lemon
One-half spoon Sugar
One-half pony of Water
One jigger Whiskey
Ice; stir well; strain; fruit

TODDIES

Toddy: A general name for alcoholic liquor. Specifically and as herein applied, a beverage made of spirits, sugar and water, the latter usually hot, and sometimes with other ingredients for flavoring.

APPLE TODDY COLD — Dissolve one lump of Sugar in three teaspoonfuls of Water (whiskey glass)
One jigger Apple Whiskey
One lump Ice
Serve with spoon and Nutmeg

(For Hot Apple Toddy, use larger glass and fill with hot water. Do not heat the Whiskey before mixing, and leave out the ice.)

BRANDY — One-half lump Sugar
Three spoons Water
One jigger Brandy
One lump Ice (whiskey glass)
Small spoon

BRANDY (Hot) — One teaspoon Sugar, dissolved in boiling Water
One wine-glass Brandy
Fill two-thirds with boiling Water
Grate Nutmeg on top

HOT BAKED APPLE — One lump Sugar, dissolved
One-fourth Baked Apple
One jigger Apple Whiskey
Fill two-thirds with hot Water

HOT WHISKEY — One lump Sugar, dissolved in hot Water

One jigger Whiskey
Fill two-thirds with hot Water

KENTUCKY   One-half lump Sugar
                Two spoonfuls Water
                One jigger Kentucky Whiskey

PEPSIN   One-half lump Sugar
                Two dashes Pepsin Bitters
                One jigger Whiskey
                One lump Ice
                Fill from siphon

OTHER MIXED POTATIONS

ABSINTHE   One jigger Absinthe (star)
FRAPPÉ   Ice; shake well; strain
                Fill with plain Water

ABSINTHE   One jigger Absinthe
FRAPPÉ   Ice; shake well; strain
(California)   Fill from siphon

ANGEL'S BLUSH   Two-thirds Benedictine (pony)
or KISS   One-third Cream

ANGEL'S   One-third Maraschino (pony)
DREAM   One-third Cream
                One-third Crème Yvette

ANGEL'S TIT   Two-thirds Maraschino (pony)
                One-third Cream

APRICOT   Cup one small Lemon
SAM WARD   Put in cocktail glass
                 Fill with fine Ice
                 Fill with Apricot Brandy

AUTOMOBILE   Juice one-half Lemon or Lime
                 One jigger Gordon Gin
                 Two lumps Ice (Collins glass)
                 Three sprigs Mint
                 One bottle Ginger Ale
First concocted in the days when the automobile was
a novelty. The fact that its alcoholic content was modest,
inclines one to the belief that it was not invented by the
victim of a motor car.

BABY TITTY   One-third Anisette (sherry glass)
                 One-third Crème Yvette
                 One-third Whipped Cream
                 Serve with Cherry on top

BISHOP   Two jiggers Water
(pitcher)   Four spoons Sugar
                 Juice one-half Lemon
                 One jigger Jamaica Rum
                 One bottle Claret
                 Ice; fruit well

BORDELAISE   One pony Kirsch (lemonade glass)
                 One-half pony Raspberry Syrup
                 Ice; shake; strain; fill from siphon

BRADLEY   Pony of Crème de Menthe on Ice or
MARTIN   plain with Crème de Cacao on top
After the husband of a famous society leader who

gave a much publicized ball in the room adjoining the
Old Waldorf Bar, while the latter was still building.

BRANDY AND GINGER ALE FRAPPÉ	One jigger Brandy (Collins glass) Fill with fine Ice Shake well; strain; fill with cold Ginger Ale
BRANDY CHAMPERELLE	One-third Curaçao (pony) One-third Boker's Bitters One-third Brandy
BRANDY FLOAT	Fill whiskey glass two-thirds with Seltzer Float pony of Brandy on top by using spoon
BRANDY SCAFFA	One-half Maraschino (pony) One-half Brandy Two dashes Angostura on top
CAFÉ KIRSCH	White of one Egg (claret glass) One-fourth spoon Sugar One pony each, Brandy, Kirsch-wasser and Coffee Ice, if preferred cold Shake well; strain
CASCADE	One pony Crème de Cassis (goblet) One pony French Vermouth Fizz with Seltzer
CHOCOLATE CREAM PHOSPHATE	Yolk one Egg (Collins glass) One pony Kirsch One pony Cream

Three dashes Acid Phosphate
Shake well; strain; fill with plain
Soda

CIDER NECTAR   Juice one-half Lemon
(one quart)   One spoon Sugar
Jigger each Brandy and Sherry
Ice; one quart Cider; Mint on top

CONCLAVE   Juice one Orange (goblet)
One pony Raspberry Syrup
Fill with chilled Milk; little Sugar;
shake; strain

CREAM PUFF   One-half spoon Sugar (lemonade
glass)
One pony Cream
One jigger St. Croix Rum
Ice; shake well; strain; fill from
siphon

CREOLE LADY   Two Maraschino Cherries
One pony Maraschino
One sherry glass of Bourbon
One sherry glass of Old Madeira
Mix thoroughly with spoon—no Ice

DELGARCIA   Fill glass with Brandy (pony)
One slice Lemon laid flat on top
One lump Sugar on top of that—
no Ice

DURKEE   One whole Lemon (Collins glass)
One spoon Sugar, muddled well

One jigger Jamaica Rum
Ice; fill with Soda; stir

EGG-NOG   One-half spoon Sugar (goblet)
One Egg
Fill three-quarters with Milk
Add Rum, Brandy, or Whiskey
Shake well; Nutmeg on top

FASCINATION   One-third White Curaçao
Two-thirds White Absinthe
One piece of Ice in champagne glass
Fill from siphon

FIN DE SIÈCLE   Tom Collins, with Grenadine and
Raspberry Syrup
      Name dates it back to 1899 or 1900, when the term
was much used, but much mispronounced.

FLAMBEAU   Cup small Orange—turn inside out
One lump Sugar
One jigger Brandy (champagne
glass)
Set fire—burn five or ten seconds

FLORADORA   Juice one Lime (Collins glass)
One-half teaspoon Sugar
One-half pony Raspberry Syrup
One jigger Gin
Frappé; fizz with bottle Ginger Ale
      After an English musical comedy that had a long run
at the Casino early in the century, and was famous for
its sextette, and for the number of wealthy marriages
made by the members of the latter.

GARDEN   One-half pony Crème Yvette
OF EDEN   One-half pony Apricot Brandy

GENERAL   One-half Lemon, muddled with
HENDRICKS   Two lumps Sugar in goblet
                One jigger Bourbon Whiskey
                Fill with chilled Apollinaris

GIN BUCK   One drink of Gin
                One Lemon in Collins glass; Ice
                One bottle imported Ginger Ale

GOLDEN   One-fourth yellow Chartreuse
SLIPPER   One small Egg (sherry glass)
                Fill with Eau de Vie de Dantzig

HAPPY   Equal parts, in claret glass of cracked
THOUGHT   Ice, of following:
                Anisette, Crème de Cacao,
                Crème de Rose, Crème de Menthe,
                Crème Yvette and Cognac

JIM RENWICK   Rind of one Lemon
                One jigger Whiskey
                Two lumps Ice (Collins glass)
                One bottle imported Ginger Ale

JOHN COLLINS   Juice one-half Lemon (Collins glass)
                One-half spoon Sugar
                One jigger Holland Gin
                Ice; shake; strain; fill with plain
                  Soda
        One of two members of the Collins family famous

in bars in the old days. The difference between the two was that a Tom Collins was made with Old Tom Gin— or supposedly—while a John Collins was made with Holland Gin.

JOHN FRAZER	Seven-eighths pony Maraschino One-eighth Angostura Bitters
JOKER	One-fourth sherry glass each, Anisette, Crème Yvette, Benedictine and Cream
JONES LA POUSSE	Two-thirds Yellow Chartreuse One-third Cream (pony)
KING CHARLES	One pony Maraschino One jigger Tom Gin Three small lumps Ice (goblet) Fill with plain Soda; Fruit
KNICKERBINE	One-third sherry glass Crème de Rose One small Egg Yolk One-third Benedictine One-third Kümmel Three dashes Orange Bitters on top
KNICKERBOCKER	Juice one-half Lemon (Collins glass) One lump Sugar Two dashes Angostura Bitters One whole Lemon Peel One jigger Brandy Fill with plain chilled Soda

After a well known New York Club, then situated
a few steps from the Waldorf, and supposed to have
been originally compounded for members of that or-
ganization, as was the case with Knickerbocker Punch
(*q. v.*).

LALLA ROOKH   One pony Vanilla (lemonade glass)
               One-half jigger Brandy
               One-half Jamaica Rum
               One-half spoon Sugar
               One tablespoon Whipped Cream
               Ice; shake well; strain

LAWYER'S   One-fourth spoon Sugar
REVENGE   Piece of Orange Peel
               One-half jigger Water; mix well
               Fill mixing glass with Ice
               Put over it jigger Port Wine
               Serve in star glass; add dash of
                 Vichy

LEMONADE   Equal parts of Raspberry Syrup,
(*à la Taylor*)   Strawberry Syrup, Pineapple
               Syrup, Lemon Juice, Currant or
               Blackberry Syrup and Orange
               Juice, with small pieces of Banana
               Ice; fill glass with sparkling Water

LOENSKY   Two-thirds pony Russian Kümmel
               One-third Scotch Whiskey—no Ice

LUNE DE MIEL   One-third sherry glass White Cacao
               One-third Parfait d'Amour

Yolk of one Egg
One-third Kümmel Doré
Oftener drunk than correctly pronounced.

MAMIE   Juice one-half Lime (Collins glass)
GILROY   One dash Hostetter Bitters
                 One jigger Scotch Whiskey
                 One bottle chilled Club Soda

MAMIE   Juice one-half Lime (Collins glass)
TAYLOR   One jigger Scotch Whiskey
                 One bottle imported Ginger Ale

MARGUERITE   One-half Lime (Collins glass)
                 Lump Ice
                 One jigger Tom Gin
                 One imported Ginger Ale

MARTINIQUE   Two-thirds pony Benedictine
                 One-third Cream—no Ice

MINCE PIE   Three-quarters pony Crème de
                    Menthe
                 One-quarter Brandy—no Ice
     No mincemeat, no pie; only the brandy that was a
standard mincemeat ingredient in those days.

MONT BLANC   One pony Orgeat Syrup (goblet)
                 One jigger Absinthe
                 White of one Egg
                 Shake; strain; fill glass with chilled
                    Seltzer

ORANGE   Cup an Orange; turn inside out
BRANDY CUP   Serve in glass with Brandy

ORANGE   Cup an Orange
FLAMBÉE   Put rind in flat champagne glass, in-
COGNAC   side out
                 Fill with shaved Ice
                 Pour over it Cognac

ORANGE   Juice of two Oranges
SMILE   One Egg
                 Enough Grenadine Syrup to color;
                   frappé

PEACH BLOW   Juice one-quarter Lemon
                 One-half spoon Sugar
                 One-half Peach
                 One jigger Tom Gin
                 Ice; shake; strain; fill fizz glass
                   from siphon

POMPIER   One-half jigger French Vermouth
                 One-half jigger Crème de Cassis
                 Ice; fill fizz or Collins glass with
                   Seltzer
    After the French term for "fireman"; but no French
fireman would understand the usual orders that were
given for it.

QUEEN   One pony Raspberry Syrup
CHARLOTTE   One jigger Claret
                 Two lumps Ice (Collins glass)
                 Fill with Lemon Soda; stir

ROBERT E. LEE One dash Absinthe
                 Juice of one Lime

One drink of Scotch Whiskey
Ice and shake (Collins glass)
One bottle of Imported Ginger Ale

ROCK AND RYE Two spoons Rock Candy Syrup
One jigger Whiskey in whiskey glass
Serve with small spoon

ROYAL SMILE One-fourth Gordon Gin
One-fourth Applejack
One-fourth Grenadine
One-fourth Lemon Juice; frappé

SABBATH One pony each, of Brandy, Port
CALM   Wine and Black Coffee
One Egg; one-half spoon Sugar
Fill two-thirds with Cream
Shake; strain into goblet; Nutmeg

SHANDYGAFF One bottle Ginger Ale
(pitcher)   One bottle Bass Ale; mix

SHERRY   One-fourth claret glass Sherry
AND EGG   One Egg
Fill glass with Sherry

SHERRY   Egg-nog; made with Sherry
CHICKEN

SINGLE   Rickey, made with Whiskey, instead
STANDARD   of Gin, and served in goblet
   This belongs to the same period, and has an origin
similar to that of Double Standard Sour and Free Silver
Fizz.

SMALL BEER Three-fourths pony Crème de Cacao
One-fourth Cream

SNOW BALL   White of one Egg
One-half spoon Sugar (Collins glass)
One jigger Medford Rum
Shake; strain; fill with chilled Gin-
ger Ale

SOOTHER   One-half spoon Sugar
Juice one-half Lemon
One pony Brandy
One pony Jamaica Rum
One-half pony Curaçao
One spoon pure Apple Juice
Ice; shake; strain into goblet

STONE FENCE   Two lumps Ice (fizz glass)
One jigger Whiskey
Fill glass with Cider (spoon)

SUISETTE   Break one Egg in glass
Juice of one Lemon
One-third jigger Italian Vermouth
Two-thirds jigger Brandy
Two dashes Absinthe
One spoon Sugar
Frappé and fill lemonade glass from
siphon

SUISSESSE   Three-quarters jigger Absinthe
One-fourth pony Anisette
Ice; shake well; strain; fill star glass
from siphon

SUNSHINE   Juice one-half each, Lime and Orange
White of one Egg

Jigger of Gin or Whiskey
Fizz with Carbonic (lemonade glass)

SYMPHONY   Wine-glass of shaved Ice
OF MOIST JOY   One-fourth each, Crème de Rose,
                  Yellow Chartreuse, Crème de
                  Menthe and Cognac; Berries on top

THREE-   One-third each; Yellow Chartreuse,
QUARTER   Curaçao and Brandy (sherry glass)

TOM COLLINS   Juice of one-half Lemon
                  One-half spoon Sugar
                  One jigger Tom Gin
                  Ice; shake; strain; fill with plain
                      Soda

WHISKEY   Three sprigs Mint
AND MINT   One-half lump Sugar, dissolved;
                      press Mint lightly
                  One jigger Whiskey; Ice

WHISKEY   Three leaves of Tansy, or a pony of
AND TANSY   Tansy Mixture
                  One jigger Whiskey

WHISKEY   Juice of one-half Lemon
DAISY   One-half spoon Sugar
                  One pony Raspberry Syrup
                  One jigger Whiskey
                  Ice; shake; strain; fill from siphon

WHISKEY FIX   One lump Sugar
                  One jigger Whiskey
    Brandy Fix made similarly. Some added one-fourth
of a Lemon and one-half Water.

VELVET   One pint Wine (Champagne)
                One pint Dublin Stout

VICTORY   Equal parts of Irish Whiskey, Hol-
SWIZZLE   land Gin and Jamaica Rum, with
                juice of one-half Lemon; frappé
Named in honor either of Dewey's victory at Manila
Bay or of the Battle of Santiago. Swizzles were first
imported from Cuba by American naval officers.

WALDORF   Apricotine and Lime Juice, equal
FRAPPÉ   parts; frappé

WARD EIGHT   Whiskey Sour, with Grenadine

WHISPERS   Equal parts in goblet, Whiskey,
OF THE FROST   Sherry, and Port Wine
                Add Sugar, to taste
                Fruit well; Ice

WIDOW'S KISS   One-quarter sherry glass Parfait
                   d'Amour
                One-quarter Yellow Chartreuse
                One-quarter Benedictine
                White of one Egg, beaten, on top
                On the last, put slice of Strawberry
Just why the author of this drink should ascribe so
many tastes to the osculation of some gentleman's relict,
or who was the widow whose kiss was thus commemo-
rated, it has been impossible to establish. One could only
suggest that someone with an inquiring mind might
catch a widow and experiment with direct labial contact.

NON-ALCOHOLIC

CIDER NOG
One-half spoon Sugar
One Egg
Shake well; fill with chilled Cider
Stir well; serve with napkin

DUMMY DAISY
One pony Raspberry Syrup
Juice one Lime (lemonade glass)
One-half spoon Sugar; Seltzer
Ice

EGG FLIP
One-fourth spoon Sugar
One Egg
Fill two-thirds goblet with Milk
Ice; shake; strain

EGG LEMONADE
Juice one Lemon
One-half spoon Sugar
Fill with Water
One Egg
Ice; shake well; strain

EGG PHOSPHATE
One Egg
One-half spoon Sugar
Three dashes Acid Phosphate
Shake well; fill with chilled
Soda

FLORIDA SPECIAL
One drink Orange Juice
One lump Ice
Split of Ginger Ale

GRASSHOPPER One-half Lemon Juice
One-half Orange Juice
One whole Egg
One-half teaspoon Sugar; Ice

HORSE'S NECK Whole of a Lemon Peel (Collins
glass)
Ice; one bottle Ginger Ale

LEMONADE, PLAIN Juice of one Lemon
One-half spoonful Sugar
Fill with plain Water
Ice; shake; fruit

LEMON Three dashes Acid Phosphate
PHOSPHATE One spoon Lemon Juice
Fill with Lemon Soda; Stir

LEMON SQUASH Muddle one Lemon (Collins
glass)
One-half spoon Sugar
Fill with plain Soda; Ice; stir

MINT COOLER Three or four sprigs of Mint
Two lumps Ice (Collins glass)
One bottle Ginger Ale

ORANGEADE Juice of one and one-half
Oranges
One-quarter spoon Sugar
Fill two-thirds with Water
Ice; shake; strain

ORANGE LILY Juice of two Oranges
White of one Egg; Frappé

ORANGE   Juice one-half Orange
PHOSPHATE   Two dashes Syrup
                  Three dashes Acid Phosphate
                  Ice; stir; fill with plain Soda

PRAIRIE CHICKEN   See PRAIRIE COCKTAIL

SARATOGA COOLER   Whole rind of Lemon
                  Two or three lumps Ice (Collins
                      glass)
                  Fill one-half with Sarsaparilla
                  One-half with Imported Ginger
                      Ale

SELTZER   Juice of one Lemon
LEMONADE   One-half spoon Sugar
                  Ice; fill with Seltzer; stir slowly

Also the following "cocktails" (*q. v.*): Ammonia, Cider, Mountain, Soda and Prairie.

B.

AMENDMENTS

DRINKS FROM OTHER CLIMES

1. MOSTLY WITH FRENCH SPIRIT

FOR reasons earlier elaborated, the art of invention, as applied to cocktails, suffered in this country a sort of hiatus during the so-called Dry Era. Americans who traveled abroad became aware that determined efforts were being made by sympathetic foreigners to keep the American School of Drinking alive—with amendments. All over Europe, in particular, visitors from this side were assured that cocktails answering to all the old familiar names would come when called, if asked for in the proper places. Many kinds were called for, but after some sampling, few varieties were chosen again.

So far as I have been able to ascertain, Europe, during the Dark Interim, produced just one new cocktail that Americans took to and adopted. I first came across it in Rome. My host there, Commendatore Giulio Gelardi, General Manager of the Hotel Excelsior, did not, however, claim the Side-Car for Italy, and Mussolini himself was silent on the subject. Americans who make their homes abroad and so have been able to watch the March of Invention over there, trace its origin to the Ritz Bar, in Paris. The correct formula:

SIDE-CAR One-third Lemon or Lime Juice
COCKTAIL One-third Cointreau
One-third Brandy
The Side-Car is somewhat reminiscent of the Stinger, as New York knew it before the War, except that the Stinger had no fruit juice in it, and needed none, having a strong mint flavor. In English fiction dealing with the Malay States, the characters seem to be forever calling for a drink of similar name. One can scarcely read a page of W. Somerset Maugham's recently published tales without being tripped up by an order to a menial to "stengah-up" his thirsty boss or the latter's guests, who then take time off to drink. "Undoubtedly," one man was heard to say who had got as near Singapore as Paterson, N. J., "that was where we got the Stinger."

He was wrong, but not until one turned up a friend who had a friend just back from Singapore was it established that "stengah" is Malay for "half." It came to mean a drink because it seemed the easiest way for a Malay servant to gather what a Britisher wanted when in need of a half-size "spot" of his favorite beverage. So that, when Mr. Maugham's characters call for stengahs, what they get are small Scotch-and-Sodas.

The pre-prohibition Stinger was thus composed:

STINGER Two-thirds Brandy
One-third White Crème de Menthe
Frappé, and serve in cocktail glass
In the Stinger that now comes back to us from France, the Brandy and the White Mint mingle in equal proportions.

From Paris too have come since Repeal a number of

good recipes based on Brandy, or Cognac, which is France's best contribution to the category of Ardent Drink. Some of the recipes were known in the United States before the War. As all contain Brandy, I have classed them as

BRANDY POTATIONS

BRANDY AND SODA	One wine-glass Brandy One-third shaved Ice Fill with plain Soda Water
BRANDY CHAMPAGNE PUNCH	Ice in Punch bowl Small glass of Brandy Liqueur glass Maraschino Liqueur glass Benedictine Barspoon pulverized Sugar One quart Champagne One pint aerated Water Use plenty of Fruit; mix well

BRANDY
CIDER NECTAR
(pitcher)
	Pony of Brandy
	One quart Cider
	One glass Sherry
	One bottle Soda Water
	Juice of half Lemon
	Sweeten to taste
	Grate Nutmeg on top
	Add sprig of Verbena and dash
	  of Pineapple Extract, or few
	  spoons Pineapple Juice
	Ice; mix; strain

BRANDY COBBLER   One-half tablespoon Sugar in
                    Water
                    One dash Maraschino (tall
                    glass)
                    One jigger Brandy
                    One slice Orange, quartered
                    Fill with Ice; stir well; dress
                    with fruits and serve with
                    straws

BRANDY   Fill glass two-thirds with Ice
COCKTAIL   Three dashes Syrup
                    Three dashes Angostura Bitters
                    One dash Orange Bitters
                    Fill glass with Brandy
                    Twist piece of Lemon Peel

BRANDY   One lump Sugar (whiskey
COCKTAIL   glass)
(OLD-FASHIONED)   Crush in dash of aerated Water
                    One dash Orange Bitters
                    One cube Ice
                    Piece of Lemon Peel
                    One jigger Brandy; stir (spoon)

BRANDY COLLINS   Fill Collins glass one-third with
                    shaved Ice
                    One wine-glass Brandy
                    Fill with aerated Water

BRANDY DAISY   Fill shaker half-full of Ice
                    Three dashes Syrup
                    Three dashes Curaçao
                    Three dashes Lemon Juice

One wine-glass Brandy
Shake; strain; fill with aerated
Water

BRANDY FIZZ

One wine-glass Brandy
Three dashes Lemon Juice
One teaspoon powdered Sugar
Ice; fill with aerated Water;
stir

BRANDY FLIP

Fill shaker half-full of Ice
One Egg
One-half tablespoon Sugar
One wine-glass Brandy
Shake; strain; grate Nutmeg on
top

BRANDY
MORNING GLORY

Two dashes each, of Syrup,
Lemon Juice, Curaçao and
Absinthe
One-half jigger Brandy
One-half jigger Rye Whiskey
Shake; strain; fill glass with
aerated Water

GEORGIA
MINT JULEP

Three-quarters wine-glass
Brandy
Three-quarters wine-glass Peach
Brandy
Teaspoon powdered Sugar
Twelve sprigs fresh Mint
Place Mint in tall glass; add
Sugar, dissolved in Water;

add the Brandies; fill glass
with shaved Ice. Do not crush
Mint

MOSELLE CUP   One pint Moselle
(pitcher)   One pint aerated Water
                       One glass Sherry
                       One pony Brandy
                       One pony Anisette
                       Three thin slices Pineapple
                       Rind of one Lemon; sweeten to
                         taste
                       Ice; fresh Mint on top

RHINE WINE CUP   Two liqueur glasses Brandy on
(pitcher)   cracked Ice
                       One liqueur glass Orange Cura-
                         çao
                       One liqueur glass Maraschino
                       One quart Rhine Wine
                       One-half pint aerated Water
                       Fruits; piece Cucumber Peel
                       Several sprigs fresh Mint; mix
                         well

SAUTERNE CUP   Two ponies Brandy on cracked
(pitcher)   Ice
                       One pony Orange Curaçao
                       One pony Maraschino
                       One quart Sauterne
                       Half-pint aerated Water; Fruits
                       Piece of Cucumber Peel; fresh
                         Mint; mix

2. CUBAN CONCOCTIONS

It was during trips to the West Indies, during the last dozen years or more, that many Americans learned a good deal about good cocktails and other mixed drinks that was not always practicable either at home or in Europe. In such beverages they often found solace, cures for home-sickness and new tastes and flavors of delightful charm, not to mention considerable potency. Most of such travelers found their ideas of what may make good drinks first broadened in Havana.

COCKTAILS

From Will P. Taylor, manager of the Hotel National, in Havana, who stuck at his post all through the recent local disturbances, which included a bombardment of his hotel, I have obtained the choicest Cuban Rum recipes. Out of compliment to Mr. Taylor, who was last resident manager of the Old Waldorf-Astoria, is placed at the head of this list the distinctive cocktail which at his hotel is also called a Daiquiri, or a Bacardi. It is served in a tall glass, instead of the flat Champagne type usual at Havana bars, and to my taste is at its best when white Bacardi is used. The recipe:

NATIONAL   Equal parts of Bacardi and Pineapple
                       Juice
                       Squeeze of Lemon
                       Dash of Apricot Brandy
                       Ice; shake; strain

Other Havana recipes follow. Cocktails should be shaken except where stirring is specified.

BACARDI DUBONNET	One-half jigger Bacardi One-half jigger Dubonnet Juice of half Lime One teaspoonful Grenadine; shaved Ice in glass
BACARDI OLD- FASHIONED	One dash Angostura Bitters Two dashes Orange Bitters One lump Sugar, dissolved in two spoonfuls Water One jigger Bacardi Serve in "old-fashioned" glass Dress with Fruit and fresh Mint
BACARDI VERMOUTH (Dry)	Half wine-glass Bacardi Half wine-glass French Vermouth Shaved Ice (Stir)
BACARDI VERMOUTH (Sweet)	Half wine-glass Bacardi Half wine-glass Italian Vermouth Shaved Ice (Stir)
BERRY	One-third mixed Orange and Pineapple Juice Two-thirds Bacardi Dash of Grenadine
BISHOP	Juice of half a Lime One-half barspoon Sugar Two-thirds Bacardi One-third Claret

BOWMAN   Crush small spoonful Sugar
BACARDI   Three sprigs Mint
                One-third Orange Juice
                Two-thirds Bacardi
    Named after the late John McEntee Bowman, Amer-
ican hotel man, who was the first to introduce modern
American hotel-keeping into Havana and who, making
the acquaintance of Bacardi on its native heath, probably did more to popularize it among Americans than
any other one person.

COUNTRY   One-half Bacardi
CLUB   One-half French Vermouth
                Dash of Orange Curaçao

CUBAN   One-half Orange Juice
BLOSSOM   One-half Bacardi
                Dash of Maraschino

CUBAN   One-fourth Orange Juice
BRONX   One-fourth Bacardi
                One-fourth French Vermouth
                One-fourth Italian Vermouth

CUBAN   Two dashes Grenadine
CLOVER   Juice one Lime
CLUB   Dash of Orange Juice
                White of one Egg
                One drink of Bacardi (white wine-
                    glass)

CUBAN   One-third Bacardi
CORONATION   One-third French Vermouth
                One-third Dubonnet (Stir)

CUBAN   Two-thirds Bacardi
LIBERAL   One-third Italian Vermouth
              One dash Amer Picon (Stir)

CUBAN   One-half Bacardi
MANHATTAN One-half Italian Vermouth
              A few drops Angostura Bitters

CUBAN   One-half Bacardi
PRINCE   One-half Italian Vermouth
              Dash of white Crème de Menthe (Stir)

CUBAN   One-third Lemon or Lime Juice
SIDE-CAR   One-third Bacardi
              One-third Triple Sec or Cointreau

CUBAN ROSE One-third Orange Juice
              Two-thirds Bacardi
              Dash of Grenadine

DAIQUIRI   One part Bacardi
              Juice of half a Lime
              One barspoon powdered Sugar
    Note: The order of adding ingredients is important.
Personal preference dictates serving the cocktail with
finely shaved ice in the glass.

DOROTHY GISH One-third mixed Orange and Pine-
                   apple Juice
                 Two-thirds Bacardi
                 Dash of Apricot Brandy

ELIXIR   Juice of half a Lime
              One-half barspoon Sugar

Two-thirds Bacardi Elixir
One-third Bacardi

FOUR DOLLARS   One-third Bacardi
One-third French Vermouth
One-third Italian Vermouth

GRAPEFRUIT   One-third Grapefruit Juice
BLOSSOM   Two-thirds Bacardi
Three dashes Maraschino

GRENADINE   One jigger Bacardi
One teaspoon Grenadine
Juice of half Lime (shaved Ice in
    glass)

HAVANA OPERA   One-half Bacardi
One-half Dubonnet
Dash of Lemon Juice
Twist Orange Peel on top

HAVANA SMILE   One-half Bacardi
One-half Italian Vermouth
A little Sugar
A little Lime Juice

HIGH-STEPPER   One-third Orange Juice
Two-thirds Bacardi
Dash of Apricot Brandy

ISLE OF PINES One-half teaspoon Sugar
One-third Grapefruit Juice
Two-thirds Bacardi

MARY
PICKFORD
One-third Pineapple Juice
Two-thirds Bacardi
Dash of Grenadine

MENENDEZ
One-third mixed Orange and Pine-
apple Juice
One-third Bacardi
One-third French Vermouth
Dash of Apricot Brandy

PARADISE
Two-thirds Bacardi
One-third Apricot Brandy

PRESIDENTE
One-half Bacardi
One-half French Vermouth
One dash Grenadine (shake or
stir)
Twist Orange Peel on top

SUNSHINE
One-third Pineapple Juice
One-third Bacardi
One-third French Vermouth
Dash of Grenadine

YACHT CLUB
Two-thirds Bacardi
One-third Italian Vermouth
Dash of Apricot Brandy (Stir)

FIZZES AND FLIPS

BACARDI FIZZ
Juice of half Lemon
One barspoon Sugar
One jigger Bacardi; Ice; shake

Strain into fizz glass; fill from
siphon

GOLDEN FIZZ   Juice of half Lemon
One barspoon Sugar
Yolk of one Egg
One jigger Bacardi; Ice; shake
Strain into fizz glass; fill from
siphon

PINEAPPLE   One barspoon Sugar
FIZZ   One jigger Pineapple Juice
One jigger Bacardi; Ice; shake
Strain into fizz glass; fill from
siphon

ROYAL FIZZ   Juice of half Lemon
One barspoon Sugar
One jigger Bacardi
One Egg; Ice; shake
Strain into fizz glass and fill from
siphon

SILVER FIZZ   Juice of half Lemon
One barspoon Sugar
One jigger Bacardi
White of one Egg; Ice; shake
Strain into fizz glass; fill from
siphon

SUNSHINE FIZZ Juice of half Lemon
Juice of half an Orange
White of one Egg
One jigger Bacardi; Ice; shake

Strain into fizz glass; fill from
siphon

BACARDI FLIP   One barspoon Sugar
                    One Egg
                    One jigger Bacardi; Ice; shake
                    Strain into a Delmonico glass

ORANGE JUICE   One barspoon Sugar
FLIP   One Egg
                    One drink Orange Juice
                    One drink Bacardi; Ice; shake
                    Serve in a fizz glass

MISCELLANEOUS

BACARDI BUCK   Two lumps of Ice in high-ball
                       glass
                    Juice of half Lime
                    One jigger Bacardi
                    "Split" of Ginger Ale

BACARDI   Juice of one Lime
COLLINS   One spoonful Sugar
                    One jigger Bacardi; Ice; shake
                    Strain into Collins glass in which
                       are three lumps Ice
                    Fill with Club Soda
                    Stir with spoon

BACARDI   One lump Ice in Collins glass
COOLER   One jigger Bacardi
                    Plenty of fresh Mint
                    "Split" of Ginger Ale

BACARDI
DAISY

Juice of one Lime
Two dashes Grenadine
One jigger Bacardi; Ice; shake
Strain into goblet filled with shaved
    Ice
Dash of Yellow Chartreuse on top
Dress with Fruit and Mint

BACARDI
EGG-NOG

One spoonful Sugar
One wine-glass Bacardi
One Egg; one glass Milk
Ice; shake well
Strain into Collins glass
Grate little Nutmeg on top

BACARDI MILK
PUNCH

One glass hot Milk
One tablespoon Sugar
Pinch of grated Nutmeg
Yolk of one Egg
One jigger Bacardi
Now, beat up thoroughly the yolk
    of Egg with the Sugar; add
    Milk, next Bacardi, next Nut-
    meg. Mix thoroughly

BACARDI
PLANTERS'
PUNCH

Juice of one Lime
One barspoon Sugar
One jigger Bacardi; shake
Strain into goblet
Fill with shaved Ice
Decorate with Fruit and Mint

BACARDI PLUS   One pony Bacardi
                Two dashes Crème de Cacao
                One dash Anisette
                Shaved Ice; stir; strain

BACARDI   Two lumps Ice in high-ball glass
RICKEY   Juice of half Lime
                One jigger Bacardi
                "Split" of aerated Water

BACARDI SOUR   Juice of half Lime
                One barspoon Sugar
                One jigger Bacardi; Ice; shake
                Strain into a Delmonico glass
                Dress with Fruit

BACARDI   Crush half lump Sugar with little
TODDY   Water in "old-fashioned" glass
                One lump Ice
                One jigger Bacardi
                One Lemon Peel (Stir)

BRUNSWICK   Juice of half Lime
SOUR   Barspoon Sugar
                Jigger Bacardi; Ice; shake
                Strain into Delmonico glass
                Dash of Claret on top; Fruit

CUBA LIBRE   Half portions of Bacardi and Coca
                    Cola

GROG   Two quarts Bacardi
                Two pounds Sugar

Two quarts Formosa Oolong Tea
When serving, dilute one-half with
very hot Water in which Sugar
has been dissolved and put slice
of Lemon in glass

MOJITO

Same as Bacardi Rickey, with little
Sugar and few sprigs of Mint
added

MORNING
STAR

One spoonful Sugar
One Egg
One-half jigger Bacardi
One-half jigger Port Wine
One glass Milk; Ice; shake well
Strain into a Collins glass
Grate little Nutmeg on top

NIGHTCAP

One-third Orange Curaçao
Two-thirds Bacardi
Yolk of one Egg; Ice; shake
Strain into white wine-glass

PEACH

Teaspoon powdered Sugar (tall
glass) dissolved in Water
Fresh crushed Mint
Juice of two Lemons
Three jiggers Bacardi
Layer of shaved Ice in glass
One whole pitted fresh Peach
Another layer shaved Ice
Dress with Mint; serve with straws

3. JAMAICAN JOLLIFIERS

Rum, Rum, Jamaica Rum!
Who in thy praise is dumb?
The strong, the weak, the gay, the glum—
All call thee good, Jamaica Rum!
—Old Song

It is recorded in Rupert Hughes—or somewhere—that the Father of His Country so highly esteemed Jamaica Rum that he once swapped a perfectly healthy negro slave for a cask of it. That, somehow, makes one recall a famous cartoon of the late Homer Davenport's—Roosevelt with Uncle Sam tapping him on the shoulder and saying, "He's good enough for me!"

As a matter of fact, George Washington did not stand alone. Many of our Revolutionary and colonial fathers knew Jamaica Rum and liked it. The Pilgrim Fathers knew rum, or came to know it, and when swallowed it seemed to go down well with the Puritan conscience. For many years rum was one of the products of New England. Perhaps Plymouth Rock and Massachusetts Bay were originally attracted to it by its ancient name.

When Englishmen first discovered what could be done with cane sugar in Barbados, rum was known as "Kill-Devill," and under that guise it made its first appearance in English literature. It was said to be a sure cure for "Blue Devils." Soon it was rechristened with the Devonshire name of "Rumbullion," meaning "a great tumult"— probably a case of swapping cause for effect. In time it became the most famous product of Jamaica, its manufacture in that Island having attained such a degree of perfection by 1788 that John Hunter, a British army physician, after a careful observation of its effects, acquitted Jamaica Rum of any complicity in the ills that befell British soldiers stationed there; in substance, Hunter declared it had no stain on its character, and that it could be drunk with absolute impunity. Thereupon the British navy adopted it as its own. Still, certain British lexicographers maintain that "Rum" is an American word, coined generations before the British acquired the habit of abbreviation, from the good old Devonshire "Rumbullion."

It is to Mr. T. G. S. Hooke, for many years assistant manager of the old Hotel Belmont, in New York, but for some years past general manager of the Myrtlebank Hotel in Kingston, Jamaica, and the Tichfield, in Port Antonio, that I am indebted for the following collection of the best cocktails and other local concoctions in which the most-famed product of Jamaica finds favor among visitors from northern latitudes.

COCKTAILS

Note: Ingredients should be added in order named. Shake except where stirring is specified. Cocktails should usually be strained.

CHINESE   Fill bar glass half full of Ice
One or two dashes Angostura
Three dashes Maraschino
Three dashes Curaçao
Three dashes Grenadine
Half glass Jamaica Rum (Stir)
Add Cherry; squeeze Lemon
Peel on top

DOLORES — Half glass Sherry
Quarter glass Jamaica Rum
One-eighth glass Dubonnet
One-eighth glass Orange Juice
Dash of aromatic Pepper

FLAPPER — One-half Jamaica Rum
One-half French Vermouth
Two dashes Angostura Bitters
Sweeten to taste
Serve with Maraschino Cherry
and slice of Orange

GRENADE — Half glass Grenadine
Quarter glass French Vermouth
Quarter glass Jamaica Rum

HONEY DEW — Eight parts Jamaica Rum
Two parts Gin
Two parts Vermouth
Two parts Water
Juice of fresh Lime or Lemon,
sweetened
Crushed Ice in glass (Stir)

JAMAICA KNICKERBOCKER — Three-fourths Jamaica Rum
One-fourth Orange, Lemon or
Lime Juice
Two dashes Grenadine
Crushed Ice in glass (Stir)

JAMAICA ORANGE — Half glass Jamaica Rum
Quarter glass Italian Vermouth
Quarter glass sweet Orange Juice

Pinch of powdered Cinnamon

JAMAICA RUM   Half glass Jamaica Rum
Quarter glass Gin
One teaspoon Grenadine
Juice of one Lime or Lemon

KINGSTON   Half glass Jamaica Rum
Quarter glass Kümmel
Quarter glass strained Orange
Juice
Dash of Pimento Dram

LIFE-SAVER   One-half Jamaica Rum
One-half Orange Juice

MAREE   Half glass Jamaica Rum
Half glass sweetened Lime or
Lemon Juice
Dash of Bitters
Bit of grated Nutmeg

PLANTER'S   One-third Jamaica Rum
One-third Orange Juice
One-third Lime or Lemon Juice
Serve with crushed Ice

QUEEN   Five parts Jamaica Rum
ELIZABETH   One part Lime or Lemon Juice
One part Grenadine

RUM AND   Half glass Jamaica Rum
FRUIT   Quarter glass sweet Fruit Juice
One teaspoon Kümmel
One teaspoon Benedictine

Two teaspoons Lime or Lemon
Juice

RUM CRUSTA   Prepare glass thus:
Moisten edge in Lemon, dip in
  powdered Sugar
Cut ends from a Lemon; peel rest
  like an apple; put rind inside
  glass so that it lines the latter
Fill shaker with Ice
Three dashes plain Syrup
Three dashes Maraschino
Two dashes Angostura Bitters
Juice of quarter Lime or Lemon
Half glass Jamaica Rum
Shake; strain into glass
Fruit; serve with spoon

SEPTEMBER   White of one Egg
MORN   Juice of half Lime or Lemon
(Jamaica)   One teaspoon Grenadine
Half glass Jamaica Rum

TEA TIME   Half glass Jamaica Rum
Half glass cold Tea
Dash of Lime or Lemon Juice
Sweeten as desired

VOLCANO   Heaping   teaspoon   granulated
  Sugar, dissolved in Water
One-half glass Jamaica Rum
Juice of Lime or Lemon (Stir)
Fill with crushed Ice and stir again

WINTER   Two-thirds glass Jamaica Rum
                  Juice of one Lime or Lemon
                  Sugar to taste
                  Teaspoon of Ginger Brandy and
                      Pimento Liqueur
                  Two dashes Angostura Bitters

PUNCHES

CARIBBEAN   Two quarts Jamaica Rum
FISH-HOUSE   One quart Brandy
                  Four ounces powdered Sugar
                  Juice of twelve Lemons
                  Liqueur glass Maraschino
                  Large wine-glass Peach Brandy
                  Ice; mix well; Fruit

COLD RUM AND   One-third pint Lime or Lemon
BRANDY   Juice
                  Twelve ounces Sugar, dissolved in
                      Water
                  Half pint Brandy
                  One gill Peach Brandy
                  One gill Jamaica Rum
                  Two and one-half pints Ice Water
                  Add Ice; mix

HOT RUM   One pint Jamaica Rum
                  Half pint Brandy
                  Half wine-glass Kümmel
                  Half wine-glass Benedictine
                  Peel of one Lemon
                  Peel of one Orange
                  One sliced Orange

One sliced Lemon or Lime
Sweeten to taste
Add three pints boiling Water
Stir up well

JAMAICA MILK   Fill shaker with Ice
One tablespoon plain Syrup
Quarter glass Jamaica Rum
Quarter glass Brandy
Fill with rich Milk
Shake; strain; serve in tumbler
    with grated Nutmeg on top

JAMAICA PUNCH   Fill shaker with Ice
One tablespoon plain Syrup
Juice of half Lime or Lemon
Half glass Jamaica Rum; shake;
    strain

MISSISSIPPI   One small glass Brandy
PUNCH   One-half glass Jamaica Rum
One-half glass Bourbon Whiskey
One and one-half tablespoons
    Sugar
Mix well; pour into tumbler; fill
    with shaved Ice; add small
    pieces of Orange or other Fruits

MYERS'   One part Lime Juice
PLANTER'S   Two parts Sugar
PUNCH   Three parts Jamaica Rum
Four parts Water and Ice
Dash of Angostura Bitters
Shake well

OLD NAVY PUNCH	One quart Jamaica Rum
	One pint Brandy
	Three pints Champagne
	Two-thirds pint Lemon Juice
	One and one-half pounds Sugar
	Juice of three Oranges
	One gill Peach Brandy

MISCELLANEOUS

BLACK STRIPE	Dissolve teaspoon Honey in little hot Water
	Cool; add three lumps Ice
	Half glass Jamaica Rum
	Fill with cold Water
	Grate Nutmeg on top
	(Same as a hot drink made by using boiling Water)
CLARET CUP AUX CERISES	Crush pound of red or black Cherries
	Cover with quarter bottle Jamaica Rum
	Let stand several hours in cool place
	Add two bottles Claret (or three)
	One sliced Orange; thin Lemon Peel
	Ice; add aerated Water
EGG-NOG BALTIMORE	One fresh Egg
	One teaspoon plain Syrup
	Quarter glass Madeira

Quarter glass Jamaica Rum
Fresh Milk
Ice; shake; strain into tumbler
Grated Nutmeg on top

EGG-NOG   Fill shaker with Ice
JAMAICA   One fresh Egg
                  One teaspoon plain Syrup
                  Half glass Jamaica Rum
                  Fill with rich Milk
                  Shake well; strain into tumbler
                  Grated Nutmeg on top

EGG-NOG   Fill shaker with Ice
MYERS   One fresh Egg
                  One teaspoon plain Syrup
                  Quarter glass Brandy
                  Quarter glass Jamaica Rum
                  Fill with rich Milk
                  Shake well; strain into tumbler
                  Grated Nutmeg on top

HOT SPICED   Two teaspoons Sugar, dissolved in
RUM   boiling Water
                  Half glass Jamaica Rum
                  Piece of Butter, walnut-size
                  Teaspoon mixed Spices (Cinna-
                      mon, Cloves, etc.)
                  Fill glass with boiling Water
                  Slice of Lemon on top

JAMAICA   Make Tea; before it becomes bit-
COLD TEA   ter, strain into jug and let grow
                  cold.

Put in tumblers, one for each
person
One teaspoon Prune Syrup
One teaspoon Curaçao
One teaspoon Jamaica Rum
Ice; sweeten to taste; fill glasses
from jug

JAMAICA   Two lumps Ice
HIGH-BALL   Half cocktail glass Jamaica Rum
                 Fill from siphon
                 Add slice of Lime or Lemon

JAMAICA JULEP   Mash half dozen sprigs fresh
                 Mint with Sugar and Water
                 Strain into bar glass; Ice
                 Half cocktail glass Jamaica Rum
                 Shake; strain into glass thus pre-
                 pared:
                 Tumbler or balloon glass, filled
                 with shaved Ice; three sprigs
                 fresh Mint, dipped in powdered
                 Sugar, and leaves upward
                 Now decorate drink with Berries,
                 Pineapple, Banana, Orange or
                 other fruit

JAMAICA   Juice of six Oranges
ORANGE CUP   Half pint Water
                 Sweeten; put in jug with
                 Half tumbler Jamaica Rum
                 Two teaspoons Essence of Orange

Let jug stand on Ice one hour
Serve, filling glasses with aerated
  Water

JAMAICA   One pint Jamaica Rum (tall
SWIZZLE   pitcher, or jug)
               Juice of six Limes or Lemons
               Six small cubes Ice
               Four spoons Sugar
               Few sprigs fresh Mint
               Use swizzle stick, rolling top be-
                 tween hands until mixture
                 froths and outside of pitcher
                 frosts

RUM-ADE   Two tablespoons Jamaica Rum
                 in glass of Lemonade

RUM DAISY   Dissolve little Sugar in Water in
                 shaker; Ice
               Juice of half Lime or Lemon
               Quarter glass Curaçao or Yellow
                 Chartreuse
               Half glass Jamaica Rum
               Shake; strain; decorate with fruit;
                 serve with spoon

RUM RICKEY   Two lumps Ice in tumbler or tall
                 glass
               Squeeze half Lime or Lemon
               Half cocktail glass Jamaica Rum
               Fill with chilled aerated Water;
                 serve with spoon

RUM SANGAREE   Spoonful Sugar, dissolved in
small wine-glass Water
Pour into large tumbler or tall
glass
Fill up with Jamaica Rum and
Water in desired proportions
One or two lumps Ice; serve with
spoon

RUM SOUR   Fill shaker with Ice
One teaspoon plain Syrup
Juice of half Lime or Lemon
Half cocktail glass Jamaica Rum
Shake; strain; splash of Soda
Water on top
Fruit

RUM TODDY   Dissolve Sugar in Water in small
(cold)   tumbler
Ice
Half cocktail glass Jamaica Rum

RUM TODDY   Dissolve Sugar in hot Water in
(hot)   small tumbler
Half cocktail glass Jamaica Rum
Slice of Lemon on top

TEA COBBLER   One teaspoon plain Syrup in
shaker
Teaspoon Pineapple Syrup, or
Curaçao
Half cocktail glass Jamaica Rum
Ice; shake; strain into tumbler

filled with cracked Ice; decorate
with sliced Fruit; serve with
straws and spoon

WHITE LION   Juice of half Lime or Lemon
Quarter glass Raspberry Syrup
Quarter glass Curaçao
Half glass Jamaica Rum
Shake, strain into tumbler filled
   with shaved Ice
Fruit

THE OLD WALDORF BAR
1897–1919
" And drop upon its grave a tear."

NOT far from the spot where the Indian chief who
sold Peter Minuit the Island of Manhattan coined
the expression, "Here's how!" when he tackled the bottle
of rum that the crafty Dutchman threw after his twenty-
four dollars to bind the bargain; not far from that spirituous spot, in later years, arose a mighty hotel. In one of
its great halls, disciples, if not descendants, of the noble
red man were wont to assemble every afternoon, and to
preface, as well as conclude, with his utterance on that
memorable occasion, deals which caused the original New
York real estate speculation to dwindle to the proportions
of a fly-speck.

What some of those men did, under the influence of a
just-ended session of the Stock Exchange, of the news-
ticker that kept discharging its tape into a waste-basket,
and possibly—and probably—of what was dispensed in
that hall by a dozen talented bartenders, helped make
American history. Men staked fortunes there; they formed
pools; they plotted to corner markets. For years the names
of certain of them made the first page of the newspapers
almost every day. They were, in their way, giants, and
they took their ease in a Gargantuan way.

Many of that noble army of gallant drinkers I knew
by name; many others I knew by sight. The majority

have gone. The great hall where they exercised elbows and appeased arid appetites every day, some of them for more than twenty years, ceased to function one dark day in June, 1919. While the light holds, let me try to recreate it, and to limn the shapes of some of those who went surging in and out, while, above the roar of conversation and the chatter of the ticker, the air was rent with calls of "Same here!" and "Here's how!"

On the walls are a few paintings—expensive-looking. Here and there is a piece of massive, if not always ornamental, statuary. In one corner stands a great rectangular counter, behind which a dozen men in white coats are busy all afternoon and evening ministering to an endless array of thirsts.

The crowd surges in. Everyone struggles to get a foothold on a brass rail that runs around the bottom of the bar. Sometimes the gang is ten deep, all pressing toward that common goal. On every face is written strong resolve. Each man pushes forward until some drinker who has been monopolizing a coveted spot falls or otherwise gives way; and then, with something like a shout, the late-comer, if he is a good squirmer or ducker, wiggles into the place thus vacated, to claim the drink he yelled for while still a Sheridan's ride away.

It should be stressed that the scene described was typical only of hours when the room was overcrowded, as it frequently was toward six o'clock of an afternoon, when men would come in who acted as if they had only one aim in life, and that was to get outside of a drink, and with no delay. Frequently, as intimated, their chances improved when some "tank" at the barside had filled to overflowing and had to be either carried or led away.

But, be it also emphasized, that Bar was not regarded as a place of "ill-repute." In its early days, particularly, men of the highest reputation frequented it; some never went from their offices downtown to their homes without calling in for at least an appetizer—or something to make them forget the worry or turmoil of the day's work. Anybody could look in, and most every man who entered the Waldorf-Astoria in those days did look, at least once. It was known all over the country; in mining camps from Mexico to Alaska, it evoked recollections of tastes and odors that parched many a throat. As a matter of fact, its fame was world-wide.

Visitors to the Old Waldorf during its latter days found difficulty, did they seek to recreate the picture of that great hall where Bacchus so long drew his greatest throngs of pilgrims and devotees, and where such, in turn, drew inspiration of the widest spirituous variety. On the spot mostly occupied by the great bar counter, a humidor had been built, and ex-tanks who came and looked through a once popular doorway often could not remember which was the proper direction to cast their sighs of regret. The back entrance from the lobby—past the telephone switchboard—with its inviting facilities for gentlemen whose capacity had been stretched, had been closed, and here young women armed with pencils and typewriters were taking dictation from industrial, financial, railway and legal magnates, so classed. Across the room and against a partition were desks for various managerial heads and factotums. And when one's eye reached that partition they had embraced only half of the room where for decades the thirsty had libationed from eight in the morning until closing time. The second part of the great oak-wainscoted

hall had been converted into a bus station, and there one
bought tickets for Montclair, the Oranges, and other points
in New Jersey, or else for New Haven and other way sta-
tions to Boston.

Some of the decorations of the temple remained. For
example, two great Egyptian-like bronze figures still stood
one on either side of the private entrance to the Jade Room,
which did not look like a door at all until you found the
handle—not easy for one who had lingered over his liquor.
Then there was still one picture, "The Ballet Dancer,"
which in that long-past age referred to probably inspired
more toasts than any other single painting in the world;
which turned more men in the direction of art-connoisseur-
ing than any other example of high art known, and whose
legs and lingerie caused far more comment and centered
more scrutiny than all the cigarette pictures of stage fa-
vorites in tights that used to help sell "coffin nails," as
they were termed, during the days when "The Ballet
Dancer's" reign was being established. On the opposite
wall hung a big copy of Paolo Veronese's "Wedding at
Cana, in Galilee," for contemplation by those whom liquor
put or left in an attitude proper for the contemplation of re-
ligious subjects. High above the paneling still hung some
of the elks' heads with which the late George C. Boldt,
long the old hotel's proprietor, had adorned the place.

But when that laboratory of Bacchic endeavor was in its
heyday, pilgrims came from far and wide—from all cor-
ners of the globe. They flocked about the rectangular Bar
counter and drank deeply of what was good stuff, if not
wisdom. As soon as the first bartender appeared in the
morning, before even arranging the multitude of glasses
of various sizes and shapes on the high stand that took up

the central space of the rectangle, he must satisfy the de-
mands of at least half a dozen accumulated patrons, either
for breakfast appetizers or for something to take away what
was left of the jag of the night before. From five o'clock
in the evening until eight, the room was jammed at its
tables and at its counter, and late-comers, whose "innards"
were sending out an SOS, found themselves impeded
in their progress toward satisfaction by S.R.O. conditions.

During those three hours named, the Waldorf-Astoria
Bar was Wall Street moved bodily uptown for an ad-
journed session of the Stock Exchange, with men betting
on how stocks would perform the next day. In one discreet corner a ticker kept clicking off news. Here market
pools were often formed. Here were to be found men
who were willing to bet on anything, and to any amount.
Financiers and market operators, with names that gained
newspaper front pages every day or so, clustered about the
tables, or joined in the maggot-like surge that squirmed
for a foothold on the substantial brass tradition that ran
along the bottom of the counter. Some who once gained
such a post of vantage never left until the Bar closed.

Many forms of beverage dated their origin to the inspiration of some clever Waldorf bartender. Or, perhaps,
it was a translation of the passing fancy of a patron who
wanted something different to drink, and entirely of his
own conception. If the result met his expectations, he
might thereafter call only for his own cocktail, or whatever it was, and the bartender, out of compliment, would
christen the new drink after its godfather.

A school of drinking, and a distinctive one, the old Waldorf Bar undoubtedly was. And—which may surprise many
—it was a real school of art—a school in which more than

one connoisseur who has since spent hundreds of thousands in collecting paintings and sculpture, got his first tuition from the pictures on the Bar walls, whose appeal was often emphasized by the cumulative influence of cocktails or highballs.

More than one middle-aged or elderly American who has survived the era that saw bootlegging grow into one of our most important industries, has reason to remember gratefully at least one feature of this particular American School of Drinking, and in which, perhaps, it was preëminent among institutions of similar learning. This was the free lunch table. There are many rich men in this land today, who, were they frank, could date their first acquaintance with Russian caviar to that generous board. There, too, many of them first learned of the superb succulence of Virginia "vintage" ham. As a matter of fact, the exoteric could there give the "once-over" to delicacies they had never before seen—or even imagined. No menu in puzzling French to mystify or confuse. The uninitiate saw what he saw, and what he fancied he could sample at his leisure. And spread out for his delectation—for he was free to choose, and to whatever extent—were light and savory canapés, thirst-provoking anchovies in various-tinted guises, and other delicacies; and there were substantial slices of beef or ham, ordinary as well as Virginia, and a wonderful assortment of cheeses of robust odors; not forgetting the crisp radishes and sprightly, delicate spring onions, and olives stuffed and unstuffed.

The temporary addicts of the lunch table were never disturbed, or rarely. Their meal ticket depended merely upon good conduct—supported, of course, by a good front. The occasional investment of a quarter in a bottle of beer

—not necessarily spent before an attack upon the lunch table—served to keep them in good standing. By such an outlay as little as three times a week, a man could eat daily from that hospitable offering a luncheon that, served in one of the hotel's restaurants, would have set him back a good two dollars—and get away with it. And many so did. The table in the Waldorf-Astoria Bar cost the hotel more than seventy-five hundred dollars a year. It proved excellent advertisement, for no inconsiderable slice of the hotel's profits came from the sale of wines and liquors.

Service was rendered with a distinction many establishments of a similar nature lacked. For example, in its early days, a small, snowy napkin went with each drink, enabling a patron to remove certain traces from his mustache or his whiskers—heavy mustaches and whiskers were abundant—without toting home odors in his hip pocket, or wherever he carried his handkerchief. And while questions were not usually asked, men who bought drinks were supposed to be able to freight them away intact, and not to spill them, or to show other effects than a certain mellowness and good fellowship—though perhaps fluency in argument or reminiscence might be forgiven one who was standing treat. In brief, a gentleman was supposed to be larger than what he drank. The theory of the proprietor of the establishment was that all his patrons were gentlemen. And the theory was good, even if it didn't always work out in practice.

The actual bar itself, a large, rectangular counter at the northeast corner of the room, as noted, had a brass rail running all around its foot. In its center was a long refrigerator topped by a snowy cloth and an orderly arrangement of drinking glasses. At one end of this cover stood a good-sized bronze bear, looking as if it meant business; at the other end, a rampant bull. Midway between them was placed a tiny lamb, flanked on either side by a tall vase of flowers. The whole decoration was a more or less delicate compliment to the heaviest patronage of the room at cocktail-time, wags claiming that the flowers were all the lamb—the innocent public—got after Wall Street's bulls and bears had finished with him.

To name the important figures that were to be seen at various times in that Barroom during its first fifteen or twenty years would be like setting down most of the names from various editions of Who's Who in America—excepting, of course, always preachers—and including a good-sized list taken from the British Who's Who and the Almanach de Gotha. As a gathering place for celebrities, the room was one of the real sights of New York. But in recollection, one cannot stop to assign faces to a particular period. There is too nearly a sea of them.

While Colonel William F. Cody—"Buffalo Bill"—clung to the old Hoffman House as long as his friend, Ed. Stokes, was its proprietor, he used to drop into the Waldorf Bar, and there one might discover him at a table surrounded by a lot of admirers.

Cody, with his wide-brimmed hat, long mustache and goatee, and in the old days wearing a Prince Albert coat, presented a handsome figure and one which eyes seldom failed to follow.

Men liked to invite Colonel Cody to "have one" with them, and it is not on record that he ever refused. In accepting such an invitation, he followed an invariable formula.

"Sir," he would respond heartily, "you speak the language of my tribe."

John W. Gates, of "Betcha-a-million" fame, and his bosom friend, Colonel "Ike" Ellwood, appeared in the Bar, occasionally, though Gates' favorite hangout was the Men's Café, across the hall. With them when he came to New York almost invariably trailed Colonel John Lambert, sometime warden of Joliet, Ill., penitentiary, but president of the American Steel & Wire Company at the time of the formation of the Steel Trust. In the Gates aura, too, one would discover John A. Drake and the latter's brother-in-law, Theodore P. Shonts—that was before he was made chairman of the Panama Canal Commission—and Loyall L. Smith, a millionaire who had once been a Chicago newsboy. And while its owner was a strict teetotaler, the round face of Diamond Jim Brady, brass fittings salesman, gormand and dinner-party impresario, could be seen circulating among the crowd, as he buttonholed this or that "Big Feller," the orb illuminated by forty to a hundred carats of diamonds or emeralds, or sapphires, or whatnot, that glowed or gleamed from an expansive shirt-front or a particularly noisy necktie.

What now seems an almost incredible proportion of the brokers and operators in the Wall Street of twenty-five to thirty years ago—at least such as were family men—had homes in the immediate vicinity of the Waldorf, Westchester and Long Island and uptown apartments not yet having come into widespread vogue as dwelling places for Wall Street. "Cocktail-hour" drew a real majority of them to the Waldorf Bar. Whether they drank or not, there they knew they would find men they wished to see.

Many of these cocktail-hour patrons were hosts at tables. As a rule, they actually drank cocktails at that time, Martinis being most popular and Manhattans running second. That was before the "Clover Club" had won in New York temples of thirst a wide but short-lived popularity. Very few fancy drinks were served at cocktail-time. There were many customers, who would stand up to the bar with a group of friends, and before they moved away would gulp down five or six Manhattans or Martinis in succession. A big banquet in the hotel would fill the Barroom at midnight, for whatever they had had upstairs of cocktails, champagne, and liqueurs, many men must have, in those days, a nightcap. Often, it took several to get them properly "head-dressed" for bed.

Not infrequently, revolution-experts were of the company present—men who were the heads or members of organizations that stood ready, at the drop of a hat, or upon receipt of a code cable, to start up trouble in any Latin-American country, provided the price was forthcoming. Gun-running was at one time a remunerative, if sometime hazardous vocation—some spelled it "avocation"—in the Caribbean and along the West coast from Nicaragua down. One dealer in ammunition and guns owned, or leased, an island up the Hudson, which was reported to be well stocked with the latest war material of the day. This could be promptly dumped into the hold of a chartered "tramp" and headed wherever trouble was brewing.

Every gold rush was followed sooner or later by an influx of rough-looking men wearing wide-brimmed hats—and more than once, cowhide boots—and the air would resound with tales of "big strikes" and of "prospects" that promised big, and whose performances later made a big hole in many a speculative bank account. Cripple Creek, for example; Alaska, Tonopah—all paid tribute to Boldt's

Bar. And those miners wanted the most expensive drinks. Champagne was their first thought.

More than once a flood of reminiscence, developed through continuous imbibition, and the cropping up of some subject that had been, or was possibly still disputable among the men from the Still-Open Spaces, threatened trouble. At least once a swift train of events beginning with a slighting reference to the virtue, valor and discretion of "Bat" Masterson succeeded in starting a panic in the Bar, because of the sudden materialization of the subject of the reference, backed by his reputation for saying the last word, and with a "gun."

"Bat" Masterson, a United States Marshal, long famous in the Northwest, and a friend of Theodore Roosevelt, was in New York at the time, but not in the hotel, when the thing started that, after he did come in, was effective in holding up trade and leaving the bartenders on duty keeping company only with the bull and the bear and the lamb on top the refrigerator table.

At a table in the middle of the room sat six big men, some of them in wide-brimmed hats. Most of them were mining men, and they were from Butte, Montana. Of the group was Colonel "Dick" Plunkett, said to be a United States Marshal.

They were talking about gold strikes, mining conditions and individual exploits, law and order, jumping claims, and other things mining men usually discussed at such gatherings. Not a little egocentric hero-worship was voiced, but the talk was mostly of what other fellows had done; of "bad men" and shootings. And Masterson's name was mentioned as having saved the expense of a lot of hangings by using his six-shooter.

Plunkett dissented. He was emphatic about it.

"I tell you what," he said, "that fellow, Bat Masterson, has killed more innocent men in his day than anybody else in the United States!"

Whether the statement was immediately challenged or not, is not recorded. Masterson had good friends in that group. A little later, one of them made an excuse and left the room. He knew where Bat was, and he got into a hansom and ordered the driver to go there, lickety-split. And he gave a news-hot version of what Plunkett had said.

Hardly half an hour after the statement had been made, Masterson in person dramatically appeared at the main door of the Barroom. One of the men at the table caught sight of him and jumped up. The others, following his gaze, turned. Two or three right hands went to hips.

Bat, after halting long enough to achieve sensational effect, strode straight across to the group. He stopped at the side of his detractor's chair.

"Plunkett," he said, "I hear you have been talking bad about me." With the words, he suddenly dug his hand between Colonel Dick's neck and collar, shut his fist, and made as if to pull the other out of his chair.

Plunkett was conciliatory. "Sit down, Bat," he said; "sit down and have a quiet drink, and talk things over."

Then a man on his other side jumped up. "Take your hands off my friend, Dick Plunkett!" he shouted at Masterson, at the same time trying to jerk something from his hip pocket.

Meantime, the effect upon the crowd had been panicky. Immediately the identity of Masterson had begun to be whispered about. "That's Bat Masterson," men told one another. "He'll shoot on sight," some added. So before

Masterson had grabbed Plunkett's collar, a movement had started toward the exit—toward all exits, in fact. Men began pouring not only into the extension of Peacock Alley, but into the Grill Room, and the emergency lavatory at the southeast corner of the Bar, past which safety could be gained, was choked by men who merely wanted to find a quick way out, but missed the door.

Opportunities offered by the assemblage of so many men who were making easy money in mining, or in "The Street," were too pregnant to be resisted by certain purveyors of luxuries. At least one noted dealer in uncut precious stones always drifted in to scan those whose actions or talk indicated they had been lucky in the market, and he usually did a thriving business because, in those times, men who had made money on "flyers" were apt to have their lighter moments. That crafty psychologist derived considerable profit from persuading such that one way to celebrate their good fortune was to select a costly trinket for the lady in the uptown flat. And invariably in the gathering were to be discovered a full half-dozen gentlemen whose specialty in trade was either high-priced art or antiques. To their activities amid those inspirational scenes one who used to know most of the local art merchants and many of the imported ones has often dated the rise of the passion for art-collecting which became so widespread and violent during the early years of the century. More than once, however, the yearning for the acquisition of "high art" instilled—or distilled—in that impregnated, if not perfumed, atmosphere, was subjected to check and revision by experience and acquired knowledge of the subject; and more than one *nouveau* who used to brag about the "old masters" he had picked up, found excuse later on to subject his art gallery to a process of weeding.

To dismiss a recollection of a place where much rude, ungainly and uproarious story-telling was done, but where, too, so much real humor came out under the stimulative effect of generously drunk spirit, without calling to mind one of its most decorative as well as most intelligent wits, would almost mean leaving the best egg out of this rum omelet. Up rises from a table at the farther end of the room a tall, slender man whose gray mustache bears evidence that the lingering traces of good liquor may be held too precious for desecration by a pocket handkerchief.

"Private John Allen to the bar!"

And "Private" John Allen never said nay to such an invitation.

The way he used to tell it, Congressman Allen—of Tupelo, Mississippi, suh!—had dubbed himself with the title by which he was invariably known. After the Civil War he found the South overrun with generals and colonels and majors, so that at encampments of Confederate veterans, when it seemed that everybody he met had commanded an army, a brigade, a regiment, or at least a battalion, while he himself had never risen above the ranks, he concluded he must be the only private of the Confederate Army who had survived the conflict. So he chose for himself the title of "Private," and thereafter gave it distinction.

Private Allen showed up at least once a year at the Waldorf, and his visits seldom continued less than three weeks. One afternoon, his friend, Colonel E. T. Brown of Atlanta, arrived at the hotel and, suspecting the whereabouts of his intimate, sought the door of the Bar. And, sure enough, at his favorite table, the center of a group of atten-

tive listeners, sat Private John Allen. On the table was a
bottle of Old Green River whiskey. At Allen's right was a
stout man, red-faced and with a tremendous mustache of a
hue that matched. The other waved his hand and shouted,
"Come right over, Colonel Brown!" As the newcomer approached, Private John arose.

"Gentlemen," he said, "this is Colonel Brown, of Atlanta, Georgia. Colonel Brown, suh, I wish you to meet
Majah Soandso. Majah Soandso is the representative, suh,
of that wonderful, that potent, that seductive beverage—
O-l-d Gre-e-n Rivah."

Colonel Brown sat and the bottle was passed around.
Another was ordered and then another. Finally, Private
John suggested: "Let's all go down to the Hoffman
House."

A few minutes later, the party lined up at the long bar
counter of that establishment.

"Gentlemen, will you indicate your preference?" Private John's voice invited. Each named his choice in turn.
Finally the white-coated bartender reached the end of
the line.

"And yours, sir?" he said to Private John.

"You may give me, suh," came the answer in a full,
round voice that reverberated through the room, "some
of that great liquah that is considered a boon in every well-
regulated household—O-l-d Gr-e-en Rivah!"

The bartender inclined his head to one side. "I beg your
pardon, sir," he said. "I didn't quite catch that."

"I said, suh," Private John returned, "some of that
beneficent, luscious, pervasive and persuasive liquah whose
eloquence has chahmed a continent—O-l-l-d Gr-r-e-e-en
Rivah!"

"I am very sorry, sir," the polite barman now returned, shaking his head. "We haven't such whiskey and I have never heard of it. But we have Old Crow, Y.P.M.—"

"What, suh?" bellowed Private Allen. "Do you mean to t~ll me, suh, that you haven't any of that famous, soul-inspirin' liquah; the joy of every American father, the pride of every American mother, and for which American children cry instead of for Pitchah's Castoria—O-l-l-l-d G-r-r-r-e-e-n Rivah?"

"I am sorry, sir," said the barman, "but we haven't it."

"Well, by Gawd," exclaimed Private Allen, his voice this time at its highest and most reverberant pitch, "you haven't got Old Green Rivah! Well, suh, I just refuse to drink in such a low-down place. Come on, fellahs!" And he led the way out of the barroom.

The next afternoon, Colonel Brown saw Private Allen and the red-mustached major in close communion just outside the Barroom entrance. The major slipped away. Private John said to Colonel Brown, with a chuckle, "Do you know, the Majah tells me he slipped into the Hoffman House Bar, this mornin', and sold 'em seventy-five cases of Old Green Rivah. Colonel," he continued, with a wink, "how'd you like, suh, for me to send you down to Atlanta a case of Old Green Rivah with my compliments?"

VI. GLOSSARIAL

SOME THINGS MOST PEOPLE DON'T KNOW ABOUT LIQUORS

FOR the benefit of antiquarians and serious students of American *mores*—as well as for the information of those who like to know what's in a name or two, when applied to liquor—the author has deemed it expedient to append a brief Glossary, which may serve to uncork certain useful and perhaps entertaining particulars concerning spirits and other things mentioned in the Formulary portion of this book.

To begin with, take "Berries." As used in the text, "Berries," it should be emphasized, does not mean dollars—simply small fruit usually growing on vines or diminutive plants. "Mug," as employed, does not signify a face, or "to photograph," as commonly applied these days; but a container made of glass, crockery, or stone, with a handle, and used for dispensing ale, cider, or, infrequently, beer. A "lemon" is a small yellow fruit; and "lemon peel," of course, is the rind.

The word "Egg," as frequently used, should be taken in a literal and primitive sense. In the days when recipes were written down in the Old Bar Book, the term "Pittsburgh Steel Millionaire" had not yet been synonymously superseded in Manhattanese by "Big Butter and Egg Man," and at the Old Waldorf Bar "Good Egg" was synchronous and synonymous with "Fresh Egg." Whatever metaphorical or sinister sense either has come later to assume, each then meant simply a natural output of a female of the chicken species, and in fair condition. A "Nutmeg" was, and still is, the aromatic kernel of the fruit of a tree of the *Myristica* family.

"Cock's Comb" as used, meant literally what it says, however incredible to those who think only of a cow or a goat when they return to the barnyard for something to drink. As an elective concomitant, if not an ingredient, of the Chanticleer cocktail, a Cock's Comb was a ruddy, serrated, distinctive capital decoration peculiar to the masculine chicken. It was pickled or bottled as a sweetmeat in France, often with other elemental components of departed roosters, particularly what are known to high-class grocers and certain gourmets as *"Financières."* The Cock's Comb and the *Financière* are still reputed among the ultrasophisticated to possess virtues akin to those of certain simian appropriations recommended by a distinguished Slavic surgeon. Indeed, the manager of one well-known mart for rare comestibles and delicacies stoutly maintained to the writer that the combination is in great and growing demand.

"Ginger ale" is now perhaps even better known than in pre-prohibition days, so it should be unnecessary to define it, except so far as to say that "imported" ginger ale used to mean that the product had been manufactured in some other country than the United States. An "orange," of course, signified about what it does today, though "orange peel" used to mean a good deal more, as in the compendium there will be found numerous concoctions in which it was used for flavoring purposes. "Mint," a pungent herb commonly found in kitchen gardens, has long filled a noble office in certain parts of this country—particularly below Mason and Dixon's line, and most notably, perhaps, in Kentucky, though in other states great pride is exhibited by many citizens in the virtues of a compound whose recipe, they claim, has been handed down in some particular family for generations past. In recent years and in New York, it seems to have become more closely identified with the chewing gum industry than anything else. It might be emphasized that when the Old Waldorf recipes were compiled, the word "raspberry" had not become synonymous with "horse's laugh" or any other anatomical performance and the expression "give him the raspberry" had not come into common use. Nor had "strawberries" entered the realm of slang. Berries were berries and fruits were fruits. It was a simpler age.

A few processes employed by bar-mixers of the old American School, and named here and there, seem to call for some clarification.

For example, to "muddle" meant to mash and stir up one or more ingredients, and had no objective reference to the person who was getting the drink; to "cup" meant either to shape or use as a cup, or to place in the bottom of a cup or glass; to "frappé" meant to cool with ice. More frequently than not, a bartender averse to the vigorous and more than local exercise demanded by plying a cocktail-shaker achieved a similar effect by the finger-and-wrist method of gently stirring a few lumps of ice with a spoon, but, as already intimated, "stirring" was often prescribed in the formula.

With this brief introduction, one passes on to the Glossary proper. The definitions are confined to terms used in the compendium. The term "voltage," given where it is

root, lemon peel, thyme, nutmegs, cassia, hyssop, peppermint, and cloves. Imitation of Benedictine is not so much confined to prohibition history as patrons of bootleggers may have become convinced. As a matter of fact, such has been going on in France and elsewhere for generations, the average customer who did not know being satisfied if the bottle was queer and squat and bore the initials "D.O.M." Voltage, 52.

BITTERS—Beverages containing alcohol, together with a component for cathartic effect. Best known varieties: Angostura, made from the bark of a South American tree; Calisaya, synonymous with cinchona or quinine, also of South American origin; Orange; Boonekamp, made in Germany; Boker's, Amer Picon (which a stenographer rendered for me "American Pecan," but which is really a French proprietary proposition); Hostetter's, West Indies, Pepsin, Peychaud (formerly made in New Orleans); Fernet Branca, etc. So named from the usual bitter taste.

BRANDY—(Sometimes called "cognac," from a town in France noted for its manufacture.) Alcoholic liquor distilled from wine. *Deriv.*, Dutch, *brandewijn*, meaning "burnt wine." Was also made from the juice of apricots, peaches, apples or other fruit by distillation, and called liqueur. Cognac was often called for by the name of its maker, though in other days it was often referred to by the symbol printed on its label, "★ ★ ★" or "★ ★ ★ ★," as indulgers frequently proved unable to read when ready for an encore. Voltage, 53.4.

CHARTREUSE—A distillation with brandy of certain rare herbs, used as a cordial or liqueur. The name was derived from the fact that Chartreuse, like Benedictine, owed its invention to early French monks, who knew about what they wanted and got it. These monks were of the Carthusian Order, and the liqueur was made only at their monastery in the Grande Chartreuse, in the French Alps. The formula for its preparation was said to be known only to the Father Superior of the Order. When the monks were expelled from France, in 1903, they spirited the secret of its preparation to Tarragona, in Spain, whence comes an herb much esteemed by gourmets in the treatment of vinegar. Rival manufactories were then set up in France, but their product was never so good as the original brand. Some thirty years or so before their expulsion, the Carthusian monks had suffered a big loss in the destruction of their brandy warehouses, wherein was stored what was said to be the largest stock of old Napoleon brandy in existence. Even before prohibition came, as much as twenty dollars a bottle was paid in New York for Chartreuse dated 1869 or before. While the monks have kept their formula a secret, analysts have named among the ingredients of Chartreuse: balm leaves, orange peel, dried hyssop tops, peppermint, wormwood, angelica seed and root, cinnamon, mace, cloves, Tonka beans, *calamus aromaticus* and cardamom. Some of the flavor, if not virtues of the product, however, was ascribed to certain herbs which were said to grow only in the neighborhood of the Grande Chartreuse. There were three varieties of Chartreuse—yellow, green, and white. Voltage, 43.

COINTREAU—A liqueur made in France, but not well known in the United States before prohibition.

CRÈME DE CACAO—An extract of cocoa, made in France. Used as a cordial or liqueur.

CRÈME DE CASSIS—A liqueur made in France of black currants, whose voltage still causes headaches to some who recall its potency.

CRÈME DE MENTHE—A distillation of mint, or of brandy flavored with mint. Usually green in color, though there is also a white variety. By those who could not pronounce its name correctly, it was often called "green mint," or "white mint," *menthe* being the French word for "mint." It is usually made in France. Voltage, 48.

CRÈME YVETTE—An extract of violets, used for flavoring purposes; also drunk as a cordial or liqueur. Its perfume often gave it preference over the common or garden refuge of the drinking dissembler—a clove or peppermint lozenge—before the commercial discovery of halitosis. Made in New York.

CURACAO—Often mispronounced "Curacoa," especially by Englishmen. A liquor made by distilling spirits with orange peel and certain spices. Manufactured originally in Holland. Name derived from that of a Dutch island off the north coast of South America. Voltage, 55.

DUBONNET—A proprietary French bitters or tonic, one of whose ingredients is said to be quinine.

GIN—Originally a drink distilled from malt or other grain and afterwards rectified with and flavored with juniper berries. Manufactured in Holland, under the name of Hollands, Schiedam, and Schnapps. For the effect of Schnapps, see Washington Irving's tale of that sterling New Yorker of pre-war times, *Rip Van Winkle.* Also manufactured in England under various names, notably: Gordon, Booth's, Holloway's, Old Tom, Nicholson, Plymouth, House of Lords, etc. Among the lower classes of London, "gin" is alcohol, flavored with oil of turpentine and common salt. The term is often used generically for "bad liquor." In some parts of the Cotton Belt, "gin" signifies a beverage whose effects are momentarily synonymous with those produced by the saws of a cotton gin—from which it is *not* derived. The actual derivation is from the Dutch *jenever*, itself coming from the old French word *jenevre*, meaning juniper. Gin was sometimes called "Geneva," or "Geneva Water," and ascribed to Swiss invention. Voltage, 54.3.

SLOE GIN—Not to be confused with the real gin, and it should be noted that as compared with real gin, its effects are described by its first name, differently spelled. Sloe Gin is a sort of cordial made by distillation from the small, plum-like astringent fruit of the Blackthorn, or a distillation flavored with the same.

GRAND MARNIER—A cordial, or liqueur, made in France from oranges.

GRENADINE—A red syrup or cordial, said to be made from pomegranates; manufactured in France.

KIRSCH or KIRSCHWASSER—A liquor distilled from European wild cherries, and made in Germany and other central European countries.

KÜMMEL or KIMMEL—A liquor made generally from highly rectified alcohol, flavored with cumin (a plant of the parsley family) and caraway seeds. Before the War it was manufactured chiefly at Riga, then in Russia. Voltage, 33.9.

MARASCHINO (pronounced "maraskeeno")—A cordial distilled from fermented cherries and flavored with bruised pits. *Deriv.*, Italian, *marasquino*.

OJEN—A cordial formerly made in New Orleans, La.,

and flavored with absinthe.

ORGEAT—A syrup made in France from sugar, orange flower water and almonds. *Deriv.*, French, from Latin, *hordeum*, barley.

PARFAIT D'AMOUR—A red cordial whose composition was a proprietary secret, but whose name often assured those who had a slight acquaintance with French that it was a sort of love potion.

RUM—Generally, the name of any alcoholic liquor. Used as an adjective, colloquial English for "queer" or "peculiar." Specifically, an alcoholic liquor distilled from fermented molasses, or cane juice. Varieties usually named from country of origin—Jamaica, Swedish, St. Croix (West Indies), Cuban—better known as Bacardi or Santiago—and Japanese (usually called Sake and distilled from fermented rice). *Deriv.*, abbreviation of "rumbullion" or "rumbooze." The latter term is composed of the gypsy word *rom* or *rum*, meaning "good," and "booze," a corruption of the Dutch *bouse*, meaning to "guzzle," but now used as a good English word with a sinister meaning. The manufacture of rum was at one time an important New England industry, antedating that of cotton cloth. Voltage, 53.7. See "Jamaican Jollifiers."

SHERRY—Originally meant the white wine of Jerez, Spain, from whose name it was derived. Jerez was pronounced "Hareth," or "Herreth." The English corruption may have been due to excessive sibilance manifested by the original Britisher who drank a bottle and demanded more. Voltage, 19.

SODA, SIPHON, PLAIN SODA, CARBONIC, SELTZER, VICHY—Water charged with gas and discharged into a glass by pressing a lever controlling the metal vent of a siphon. CLUB SODA, aerated water in a small bottle. LEMON SODA, the same with a flavor of synthetic lemon. DELATOUR SODA, a brand of a particular manufacturer. The word VICHY was a misnomer, appropriated from that of the famous water bottled at Vichy, France, by the French Government.

SWEDISH PUNSCH—A beverage manufactured in Sweden, and having somewhat of the taste and properties of Rum. Voltage, 26.3.

VERMOUTH—A liquor made from white wine, flavored with aromatic herbs. Formerly, of the two varieties, the Italian, or sweet, was made in Italy, and the French, or *sec* (dry), was manufactured in France. A *sec* Vermouth is also made in Italy. *Deriv.*, German, *wermuth*, meaning "wormwood." In the country of its origin, Vermouth is often drunk "neat," that is to say, unmixed with water or more potent liquids. Voltage, about 17.

VIN MARIANI—A wine made in France from cocoa, and formerly very much advertised as a tonic.

WHISKEY—Again less comprehensive in definition than of late years, whiskey is an alcoholic liquor obtained by the distillation of a fermented starchy compound, usually a grain. *Deriv.*, Gaelic, *uisgebeatha*, "water of life." It used to be called also *eau de vie* or *aqua vitae*, meaning the same as the Gaelic term. The Swedes appropriated the name for "Aquavit," now one of their national drinks. Varieties: rye whiskey, made from that product; corn whiskey, called "Bourbon" if manufactured in Kentucky, and blended with rye, but turned out as "White Mule," "Moonshine" and under other names in illicit distilleries throughout the South; "Scotch," named for the country of its origin and popularly supposed to be made of oatmeal, the national dish, turned into spirits by the aid of peat fires, but more probably of barley or other grain, and "Irish," made in Ireland.

WINE—The juice of grapes, fermented by nature, in course of time. Varieties named in the compendium include Claret, the ordinary red wine of certain districts in France (voltage, 13.3); Burgundy, the heavy red wine of Bourgogne, France (voltage, 13.6); Madeira, the wine of the Portuguese Island of that name; Port, a wine whose name came from the Portuguese city of Oporto, whence it was exported; Rhine, meaning a wine made of grapes grown in the Rhine valley; Beaune, wines both red and white, made in the vicinity of Beaune, France, and about the same voltage as Burgundy; Bordeaux, made of grapes grown in the territory contiguous to the city of Bordeaux, France (voltage, 11.5); Champagne, an effervescent wine made before the war in the Marne region of France, particularly at Rheims (voltage, 12.2).

BAR GLASSES—Among the glasses mentioned as proper for the service of the fancy potations, the name "star" appears frequently. According to surviving authorities on bar-containers of the period, a "star" was synonymous with a SOUR glass.

The SOUR glass, so called because it was used for "sours" of various kinds, held from five and a half to six ounces. The LEMONADE was originally a thick goblet, but in time it became a thin, straight-sided glass, holding from six to eight ounces. The latter was originally the same as a FIZZ or a HIGH-BALL glass. The COLLINS started out by being an eight-ounce glass, but a demand for a longer drink led to the adoption of a twelve- or even a sixteen-ounce glass—one that, besides the gin and the ice, would hold a "split" of soda. The CHAMPAGNE was usually a wide-bowled, thin-stemmed goblet; often, however, a thin four-ounce tumbler, was also used, the same being also called an APOLLINARIS glass. A SHERRY glass was a small glass with a sharp, conical bowl, holding from three-quarters of an ounce to about an ounce and a third. A PONY was identical with a small liqueur glass, and held a scant ounce. A POUSSE CAFÉ glass was an elongated pony, holding about an ounce and a half. A WHISKEY was a thin, low, straight-sided vessel holding about four ounces. The CLARET, a thin goblet, held from three and a half to four ounces.

The JIGGER was a conical metal container, holding about two ounces. In many establishments its use was abandoned in favor of the barman's eye. He was supposed to be able to gauge a jiggerful when pouring from a bottle in composing mixed drinks. In first class establishments, the customer was usually permitted to measure his own whiskey when he took it "neat," or in a high-ball.

www.ingramcontent.com/pod-product-compliance
Lightning Source LLC
Chambersburg PA
CBHW021927040426

42448CB00008B/941